BURNT DIARIES BY EMMA TENNANT

BURNT DIARIES

BY EMMA TENNANT

published by

CANONGATE BOOKS

First published in Great Britain in 1999
by Canongate Books Ltd, 14 High Street
Edinburgh EH1 1TE

10 9 8 7 6 5 4 3 2 1

British Library Cataloguing-in-Publication Data
A catalogue record for this book is available on request
from the British Library

ISBN 0 86241 986 7

Typeset by Palimpsest Book Production Limited
Polmont, Stirlingshire
Printed and bound by Butler and Tanner Ltd, Frome

FOR TIM OWENS

CONTENTS

Going West

Wham! I'm lying in bed in Chelsea, in the part of
the first-floor drawing-room described by the
antiquary Christopher Gibbs as the 'dog-leg' (I've
given up my bedroom to the new baby: in a month
or two we'll move to the uncharted waters of W11) –
and a packet with pages bursting from the seams
lands with a thud right on top of me. What is it? I
pull at the contents, unaware I am handling
material so toxic that a reader at the publisher
Jonathan Cape has pronounced its creator fit for
psychiatric treatment, and has strongly advised
against its transition into hard covers. '*Crash*!'
laughs Michael Dempsey, hurler of the seditious
volume and friend of the author, J. G. Ballard.
'Crashed cars and sex – you know, the kind of thing
he likes.'

I've met Jimmy Ballard, at a party given in
this same Chelsea house. He's an enigma, from the
moment he rises up the stairs with his olde-worlde
Fifties greeting: 'You look glam, dear,' to the litany of
violence to be seen in the exhibition of crashed cars
organised with Eduardo Paolozzi at the ICA, this
spelling out a deathly acceptance of disaster.
Ballard's landscapes, whether abandoned helipads
or drained swimming-pools, have been obsessing

me lately – particularly since he has come to visit us here. Now, it appears, his own obsession with Elizabeth Taylor has set off a Celebrity Ward prose poem: a liturgical chant for fame, blood and sex on the motorway. I know he lives in Shepperton – 'the last station on the line' when his late wife went house-hunting shortly after their marriage. But his home had been in Notting Hill. I sense, when he speaks with a heavy sarcastic fondness of friends, other 'science fiction writers' (for J. G. Ballard has outpaced his peers, hailed as the discoverer of 'inner space' and can be seen as the Coleridge of their world), that it is neither Shepperton nor Chelsea that attracts him. Notting Hill – or Ladbroke Grove – as, in Ballard's words, 'the hill SF buffs have all rolled their pennies down, over the years' – is the land he wants to return to.

I have found a house backing onto communal gardens, these half-nurtured by loving residents and half a wilderness of broken glass and kids running amok. I know the district hardly at all; the tall houses with their long rows of doorbells are daunting, with the peeling stucco that looks like skin flaking off. There is – though of course it's deeply uncool to mention this – hardly a restaurant or delicatessen to be found here. Apart from L'Artiste Assoiffé, that is, up on the corner of Westbourne Grove and Kensington Park Road, which seems at first to be an eccentric's private house, with strange pieces of furniture and a shrieking parrot on a perch. I've noted Stout's in the Portobello Road, an old-fashioned grocer where food can be bought for the household. And of course there's the market. Just as much as seeing the science fiction writers promised by Ballard, I look forward to picking vegetables and exotic fruit from the barrows there. I write to my parents, safely retired to Corfu, of my imminent move to a planet where wild-eyed men with green hair will be my closest neighbours. My father writes back, worried at my decision to go to Notting Hill.

AUTUMN 1973

Wandering Chatwin

Notting Hill certainly does have its indigenous
writers. No sooner had I moved in to 60 Elgin
Crescent and strolled out the back door into the
communal gardens than I bumped into a nest of
them, by the doorway of a Ladbroke Grove flat.
Here were Michael Moorcock, burly Dickensian
looks, progenitor of time-traveller Jerry Cornelius;
John Sladek, computer genius from Minneapolis;
John Clute, walking encyclopaedia of science fiction
and fantasy – but after all these strange faces, the
writer I've most enjoyed seeing doesn't belong to
Notting Hill at all, he belongs to the world, and I
feel it's a good omen that a party off the Avondale
Road, gone to without knowing who was giving it,
yielded Bruce Chatwin.

'Where on earth am I?' might be a good way of
describing the way one feels on seeing Bruce again
after several years. For the party is in one large
room with no furniture but a brightly spotlit
shocking-pink four-poster bed; the guests are all
strangers, as far as I'm concerned, and I might have
wandered into a room in Paris (Bruce tells me,
when we've recovered from the delight of finding
each other there, that he's been to the capital of
chic, interviewing the once-famous couturier

Madeleine Vionnet). Or I might have ended up in Peru, another haunt of Bruce's – or in the apartment of a follower of Mrs Gandhi in India – Bruce has been on her campaign trail for the *Sunday Times* magazine. One of the most exhilarating aspects of being with Bruce is the way the globe spins into a fan of kaleidoscopic images as he speaks. And this evening, against the thump of the music – and conscious of receiving appraising looks from the throng, his blue eyes bright, his blond hair parted at the side like a prep-school boy's – Bruce is very noticeable indeed.

It turns out, despite the fabulous locations visited by Chatwin recently, that his principal concern is the book on nomads he writes and rewrites, never to his satisfaction. 'It's all to do with Abel and Cain,' he shrieks at me, as spiked drinks, acid and cherry-ade and vodka and as many other ingredients as the new Notting Hill swingers can dream up for their herbal concoctions, are handed round and dangerously quaffed. 'The first men were *nomadic* – Cain killed Abel because he was a farmer – he didn't *move*— ' Something like that: it's as hard now to make out what Bruce actually means as it was in the days he was at Sotheby's, and came for one of his flying visits, examining my small collection of paintings with a deadly yet irrefutable eye. Somehow, one knows Bruce must always be right: he is sure of it, and would be astonished to find himself contradicted.

We go back to my house, and Bruce confesses he has brought his pages on the nomads in his shoulder bag. In turn, I try to tell him about science fiction writers, and the pure imagination I fancifully consider to lie at the heart of Notting Hill. I talk of Ballard, who comes frequently to see me, encouraging my notion of founding a magazine. Why don't I do it, it could be, like *Blast* or *The Dial*, as sporadic as I please, he would certainly write for it – but Bruce has no interest in the alternative worlds on offer here in W11. 'I like Flaubert,' he announces grandly, as if that must put an end to the subject, and so it does. He looks interested in the idea of a magazine, though. 'The English are such *philistines*,' he mutters – for Bruce is either very shrill or very quiet indeed. Then he has flown. I am left with the nomads and read deep into the night the original, sometimes highly improbable, theories of Chatwin on the beginnings of man. After a while, the anthropological questions of my new neighbourhood begin to supplant the early tent-dwellers of Chatwin's prose, and I go to sleep thinking of the anti-Establishment figures here, in Notting Hill: Mike Horowitz in Colville Terrace, leader of the Children of Albion, inheritor of the fiery beliefs of William Blake. Moorcock again, known for writing a book in a week, full of the prophecies of a world of the future: *A Cure for*

Cancer, Breakfast in the Ruins. Ballard's *Crash*, finally, settles on my dreams as I drift off in the early hours, to the sound of blackbirds in the communal gardens at the rear and thieves breaking car windows in the crescent out in front. 'Should *Crash* have an exclamation mark after it?' in my half-sleep I hear Ballard wondering, on one occasion when he brought to the house a newly published copy of the lambasted book. I don't know I can answer that one, but, as I remember trying to enthuse Chatwin earlier with the idea of a *Blast* or a *Dial* in this place where writers pop up from under the ground, bloom and disappear in a day, Yes, how about trying to found a magazine . . . ?

SPRING 1974

A Visit from NW1

Stephen Frears comes to Elgin Crescent, from the
very different world of Camden, Gloucester
Crescent. Something serious about the Gloucester
Crescent group (despite or perhaps because of this,
Mark Boxer has turned the residents of this North
London street into a sly cartoon strip, *The
Stringalongs*) made me afraid of meeting Frears –
he'd had it suggested to him that I might write
something he could direct – but as soon as I see his
dark, comedian's face I realise there is nothing to
fear. We soon also realise, sitting at the trestle table
in the basement of No. 60, that we will never be
collaborators. Stephen has made the *spoof noir*
thriller *Gumshoe* and has made films for the BBC
written by Alan Bennett, one of the most moving
being *Sunset over the Bay*, about a retired couple in a
Northern seaside town. All this is about as far from
the world of Ballard's crashed cars, highly lit sex and
porn movie stars as it is possible to get – and, at
present at least, his is the vision of the world that
turns me on. I tell Frears of my idea for a magazine.
His gloomy face lights up. 'You should get to know
the brother of the girl I'm in love with,' he says.
'Julian Rothenstein. He'll design it for you, I'll tell
him to give you a ring.'

This is all very well, I tell myself, when the meeting has been fixed up. How on earth do we raise the money for it? And I remember my father telling me that magazines and night-clubs are a sure way of losing money: no-one should invest. As brother of David Tennant, proprietor of the Gargoyle Club, and Stephen Tennant, whose artistic life must have been like one long loss-making magazine I sadly concede my father might be right.

Inner Space

'There's something in the air, here' – Dinny, a new friend I've made since coming to Notting Hill, teases me as she stands in the doorway of an over-populated flat that spills out onto the Ladbroke Grove end of the communal gardens. She's seen my surprise at the frantic pace of life as well as the sense of timelessness, of the SF writers, musicians and out-of-their-minds poets with their Czech, American and West London girlfriends who throng the Grove and Portobello Road, ending up nine times out of ten in the noisy front room of the Moorcocks. The doorbell never stops ringing, there. The place is full of children. Yet Moorcock, with the frenzied energy of the mythical figure he has already become – a Hephaistos, hammering out the figments of the future on his anvil – writes a book in as short a time as it takes one of the new gentrifying incomers to shop for food in the market, consult a glossy cookbook and rustle up dinner in her just-installed stripped-pine kitchen. Moorcock's concoctions, worshipped by a motley crowd who pour in at all hours, are as far from respectable cuisine as it is possible to be. His chief protagonist, Jerry Cornelius, straddles time and space effortlessly, the sole territory he would never enter being that of our neighbour, the upright and disapproving mistress of her husband's Rolls. A war is in the making between the rebels of Notting Hill, with their high perches in Powys Gardens, All Saints and Westbourne Park Road, and the recent purchasers of houses in the stucco crescents. Obviously, I don't want to be lumped in with the latter group. I pretend to agree with Dinny fervently – before racing to immerse myself once more in the market, with its rails of cotton caftans, its sudden splashes of white Victorian children's dresses, starched to a deathly stiffness, and its barrows of bulging yellow peppers. There's definitely something in the air here. Even if it's usually nothing more than the sharp stink of German sausage from the mobile stall, rising to combat the lingering marijuana smell outside the Warwick Castle. It's invigorating; even if the area already suffers from the middle-class self-consciousness of newly arrived artists and film-makers who talk about being 'on the front line' when what they mean is crossing the road when confronted by a posse of black youths. (The police, of course, are upping the stakes when it comes to out-and-out war). Notting Hill, owned fiercely by so many imaginations, has a climate of its own.

But do I fit into this? Can I breathe the air without appearing a tourist, an upper-class twit? Only the exercise of the imagination will tell: 'Take my plan!' Moorcock said a few weeks back, drawing with precision in coloured inks on the lined page of a school notebook. 'Your book will be a hundred and sixty pages – forty pages introduction of characters' – he draws a red line – 'forty pages characters in their situations,' and as he spoke and mapped out my first foray into his charmed world I couldn't help wondering what Henry James would have thought, if confronted with this speedy, businesslike approach to the novel. Nevertheless I shall embark on it; there were too many manuscripts of unfinished naturalistic novels under my bed in Chelsea for me to even want to bring them, when I moved here.

As well as this, I want to start a magazine – but this often-repeated desire is inclined to meet with shaken heads and rolling eyes in the world of Moorcock. Don't they have *New Worlds*, the definitive SF magazine, already? Was I not fortunate enough to have a portion of the book I've tentatively started, *The Crack*, published by him in its pages?

A magazine is a venture not recommended in a household already overburdened with deadlines, nappies, needy guitar-players and hangers-on of all kinds. Yet, enthralled as I am by the infinite possibilities of 'speculative fiction', of the landscape of Ballard, Sladek, Moorcock and Tom Disch, I'd feel happier producing a paper that's open to realism and poetry as well. It will probably never happen. But if it's going to happen anywhere it'll be here in Notting Hill.

Royal Flush

I've rented a house, Glen Douglas in the Borders of
Scotland, in a futile attempt to re-create the
summers of the past, at my childhood home, Glen. I
have my two small daughters with me, and a friend,
Rosalind.

'It's one thing to want to start a magazine,
quite another to raise the money to fund it,' I tell
her portentously, as we continue our endless
discussions on the subject.

I had the solution come to me yesterday –
after pretty well everyone had turned down
requests for starting-up money for a literary paper. I
confide the idea to Rosalind; but the poor girl looks
dumbstruck, as if I had suggested a painful – and
painfully embarrassing – visit to a strange but
famous family (which, I suppose, is how people
would see the set-up at Glen now: my elder half-
brother organising blush-making 'soirées' with
'maids' dressed in the fake Tennant tartan, bagpipes,
risqué Scotch jokes, haggis, the lot).

'You *can't* do that!' Rosalind explodes.

'All you have to do is keep a look-out,' I plead
with her.

Without Rosalind, my plan could never work.
And after I've pointed out that she's not expected to

accompany me on an hour's drive from the house
I've rented near Jedburgh at night – so won't be
expected to attend a ball, play forfeits, strip off,
recite poems or otherwise die of shame, she
reluctantly agrees to come.

'In the afternoon. All will be over in a minute,'
I say.

Glen is enjoying one of its few days of heat
and sunshine of the year. Rosalind and I arrive, (in a
taxi – neither of us can drive) and I ensure he parks
out of sight of the main house, beyond the arch
which says SALVE or VALE in great stone letters,
depending on whether you are arriving with servant
in tow (Raine, then Countess of Dartmouth, a
frequent guest of my brother) or leaving (anyone
who has outstayed their welcome, usually a
member of the family).

As it turns out, there is no-one in the house
anyway: everyone is up at the pool, a new
showplace number of brightest Hollywood blue,
with a statue of Rob Roy looking out across the
water to the 'Children's Garden' where once, when
we were small, my younger brother and sister and I
used to play.

'Come on!' I say to Rosalind, spotting the
wandering figures of guests as they stroll to the pool
from the French windows of the drawing-room, of
this Gothic mock castle. Even the gargoyles above
our heads seem disapproving of the pool. 'It's too

good to be true,' I hiss, as I try to summon the courage for my theft.

But Rosalind is not made of the stern stuff for which her appearance prepares possible friend or foe. Behind the determined jaw and frowning brows is a girl who would much prefer to be back in North London, whence she bravely came to sample the beauties of Scotland. 'It won't take a minute,' I insist, betraying my own fear and sudden attack of cowardice.

The hall at Glen has never seemed so long, the grass-green carpet laid by my mother the only remaining sign of her and my father's occupancy of the place. (Books are replaced by books-by-the-yard, as my brother sold the Redouté volumes or the library of Madame de Pompadour, acquired by old Sir Charles a century ago. Pictures have also been sold, and only ill-executed and large renditions of forebears hang on the walls). So, in a landscape that is both alien and familiar to me – and therefore fearful – I run on leaden legs from the front hall down to the drawing-room door. It's open. A blast of lilies and phlox greets me, combined with cigarette smoke. The last guests must have gone just a minute or less ago.

The photograph albums are kept in the front of the outsized space my brother and sister-in-law have made of what was once the drawing-room and the Walnut Room, side by side. The books are new, smartly bound . . . my sister-in-law is well known for her addiction to photographs, these pored over at night after dinner and new batches stuck in in the morning. Will a suitable picture be there for me to steal?

Rosalind watches from the door as I approach an entire cemetery of white leatherised albums, arranged stiffly in chronological order, and try to pull out a volume more recent than – one glance is enough to tell how far back they go – the photos of bright rows of girls, my sister-in-law and her sisters: red-gold-haired from the same pine-forested, wide-beached part of East Anglia as the Royal Family.

These are the last pictures I want: the daughters of the late Earl of Leicester; their own sandy children, their nannies and aunts. In order to rush past the early days of my elder half-brother's marriage, the Georgian doll's house in Kent and the respectable young couples, I pull out a vast tome too quickly and it thuds to the floor. I hear Rosalind's whine of anxiety at the door – and I hear (but it could be upstairs, where another whole world, the world of the children of the house guests lives out its daily ritual as rigid as in the days when Glen was built: starched Norland nannies with glasses of cloudy milk and fingers of shortbread on willow-pattern plates, clothes horses festooned with button-up Peter Pan suits and smocked lawn dresses from Knightsbridge) – I hear footsteps, followed by

the low, urgent call I have persuaded my friend to
give if I am disturbed at my criminal actions.

It comes so easily, in that last minute between
success and disaster which all burglars must know
and perhaps crave when they are locked away for
their crimes. The album under the one that slid off
so conveniently opens to my trembling fingers at a
page as far removed from Norfolk wide skies and
the hand-me-down cottons of the Earl's non-
inheriting daughters as, say, the night-clubs of
Soho, of which I had dreamt so fervently
when an adolescent here at Glen, are from the
squat little kirk at Traquair down the road.
Even as the footsteps come closer – the hall at
Glen is long enough, I think recklessly, to allow at
least fifty seconds for the removal of the perfect
shot – I have to pause in admiration at the
arrangement of the album devoted to the pleasures
of Mustique.

Palm trees of course, one or two of them, set at
picturesque angles to show we are really in the
Caribbean here – without them one could imagine a
house party in the south of England on a hot day.
Upper-class families are sprawled on wicker chairs,
one lordling actually hurling what seems to be a
bread roll in a picture of Basil's Bar – but the shutter
has moved too fast and it's only a blur, as if a piece
of foam had been scooped up from the blue water
under the roofed jetty and tossed casually in the

direction of the photographer. Women, dukes'
daughters and ex-wives, in huge hats as if at Ascot.
Basil himself, grinning straight into the lens. I can
smell the shellfish, the rum punch and fresh lime,
and hear the steel band music . . . Like the Master
of Ceremonies he has been almost since birth, my
elder half-brother is leading a troupe of dancers in
one picture, his trademark straw hat on his head,
his handsome face smiling with that courtier's
smile, which is on the next page devoted to the
carving of a barbecued sucking-pig at Basil's Bar, a
line of English gentry waiting as if in a marquee at a
Hampshire ball. Then comes the photo I take; I
deliver it from the confines of four little grey tucks
in the stiff grey paper.

I thrust Princess Margaret – there's no time to
see if she's actually naked, but the picture gives at
first glance that impression – into my shirt, open-
necked on this fine summer's day. Roddy Llewellyn
comes into my bosom, too: he's very much in focus,
attentive, even loving, clearly an amorous couple is
what this holiday snap announces – and, as I close
the album and push the fallen one out of sight
under the piano, I turn to meet the footsteps, now
inside the door. Courteous as always, my elder half-
brother introduces himself to Rosalind; I hear her
anguished mumble and I step from the L-shaped
part of the long room into the main sweep, where
the new decor, in the shape of a family tartan

carpet, seems to dance hideously green and mauve
– a symptom, doubtless, of the nervous tension I'm
under – before my eyes. I feel the purloined photo
cut into my flesh, anchored by the top of my bra,
and I wonder, for the first time as I am ashamed to
own, whether it will really fetch the money needed
to start up a literary magazine. However, I can
hardly fish it out now, the consequences being too
extreme even to imagine.

'Would your friend Rosalind like to see the
loch?' my brother asks. He is the perfect host. All
the way up to the stretch of black water imposed on
the valley by our grandfather before the First War, I
feel the guilt, as well as the cutting edge of the
photo's hard, glossy surround, as penance for my
skin with each lurch of the family van on the
pitted road.

I've been back in London a week and it becomes
increasingly obvious that I just haven't the nerve for
this type of thing. Glamorous friends, well used to
Magnum or 'shoots' with Snowdon all over the
world, advise me crisply on the subject of selling
P. M. in *semi-flagrante* . 'Call *Paris Match*,' says
James Fox, brilliant contributor to the *Sunday Times*
magazine. 'They'll pay best.' Others say something
about Amsterdam. But I'm unable to go through
with it. Apart from wrecking Rosalind's holiday in
Scotland, what has been achieved by my foolish trip

(and expensive: the taxi took up most of the week's budget)? I take the photo from its hiding-place – a volume of Diderot – in my bookshelf at Elgin Crescent and can no longer bear to look at it. A warm late September – why would I want to light a fire? I think miserably. People would wonder what I was trying to destroy (by now I am paranoid as well as terminally guilty). Besides, another friend is kind enough to point out, photos refuse to burn on occasion. What if the police come searching – sooner or later our uninvited appearance at Glen will start to appear fishy.

When I hear the alarm has gone out about a photo missing from the famous albums (a family member passes it on) and that all the nannies then resident at Glen have been interviewed by Peebles police, I know it's time to end this. I admit it was hard not to laugh at the picture of these grim martinets lined up in a police station, accused of theft – but there wasn't much time left to laugh in. Too many people were in on the secret, in the first place: 'Flush it down the lavatory,' said an exasperated about-to-be-ex-friend, 'or something . . . for God's sake.'

The advice couldn't have been worse, as it turned out. Even after cutting the small, standard-size picture in several pieces with nail scissors, locking the door of the bathroom and consigning the fragments to the bowl, the faces and other

portions of Princess Margaret and her companion
floated determinedly through repeated flushings.
Finally, maddened and punished by their resolve
never to go down, I had to pick out the pieces and
wrap them in old newspaper before consigning
them dangerously to the bin.

*J. G. Ballard, Wm Burroughs and the Birth
of* Bananas

Despite having been turned down for a grant by a
London Arts Board, Carmen Callil on the panel,
there is now enough to start a magazine – or a
'literary newspaper', for we want it to follow Ezra
Pound's precept that 'Literature is news that stays
news.' Julian Rothenstein will design: he saw at
once the mix of irreverence, excellence in writing
and sheer wackiness that seems right nowadays –
about to be memorably summed up by Tom Nairn
in his piece 'Pardon Me Boys, Is This the Bognor
Regis Choo-choo?' for the paper. What shall we call
it? Why not *Bananas*, with Woody Allen in mind?
(Fyffes, however, refuse to advertise.) Max
Egremont, a budding writer, has contributed a start-
up £3,000, and various small donations have come
from others. Julian decides to put a grainy blow-up
of a police photo-fit of a female bomber on the
cover. Claud Cockburn will write of his meeting in
early 1920s Vienna with the great Ezra, there to
start a mag himself and 'move the cultural centre
from Paris to Vienna'. I keep expecting Claud, who
greets the birth of *Bananas* with delight, to say he'd
like to be paid in spondulicks – this is how he refers
to money, of which he is invariably short.

It looks as if William Burroughs will be the
hero of *Bananas* No. 1. Barry Miles, his follower,
annotator and Boswell, produces Burroughs
memorabilia. Jimmy Ballard, who comes here from
Shepperton more and more frequently, a few
evenings ago clad in a white suit and shades and
carrying maps (but what cartographer could satisfy
the wildest shores of his imagination?) – speaks of
Burroughs with reverence. A photo of Burroughs
pointing a gun is found. And Heathcote Williams, if
not the hero is the spirit, the Ariel of our new
Notting Hill magazine. I interview him for the paper:
'E. T. "Why do you want me to buy you a dress,
then?" H. W. "Well, we're all hermaphrodites . . ."'
Heathcote's play *AC/DC* in which the Royal Court
took out all the seating and left the audience to
stand while pelted by the puns, double and triple
entendres and sheer schizophrenic charge of the
words, ignited the '60s. Now, with his daughter
China, he is leaving his squat for Ledbury Road.

'" Dr Clock"? It shocks me,' says Max, our
backer, laughing. And it's true the poet Ruth
Fainlight's story 'Dr Clock's Last Case' is highly
pornographic. However, sandwiched between
Ballard's story 'The Air Disaster' and Ted Hughes's
strong, frightening poems, no censor has noticed
Ruth's wicked, sexy 'Dr Clock'. As for Ted Hughes: 'A
bullock of cooling black bronze . . . ' is his opening
poem, in the handful he has sent us; and it occurs

to me, as I look at the giant photo of Jimmy Ballard that Julian puts in at the side of his terrifying tale of an airliner crash with a thousand dead, that the imaginations of Hughes and Ballard seem to express the forked path of the imagination, since the Romantics and the Industrial Revolution, Ballard on the accidie of the flyover and high-rise, Hughes a faithful recorder of the violence of an unchanging countryside, bitter and tender. To accompany his poem, Julian puts an engraving of a bull by his father, the artist Michael Rothenstein. To our horror, the image of the bull grows smaller and smaller as we push more poems onto the page. 'I've shrunk my father's bull,' says Julian fearfully as we peer at the minuscule creature in our new office, a shabby room off the Portobello Road.

At No. 2, Blenheim Crescent, a house with a façade painted a bright psychedelic design and thus unmissable, as far as mad poets and would-be contributors are concerned, we have a first-floor 'office' with a large round table, a back room where the poems, already arriving in droves, sit in plastic bags, and a smart new electric typewriter, a 'golfball', which makes our pleas for distribution and our rejections more polite and official. Rosalind Delmar is on the 'staff' of *Bananas*, and other helpers are part-time. Barry Miles, who is co-ordinating the sending of the magazine to American universities, sits in the front room, throwing out anecdotes of Ginsberg, the Beats and, always, Burroughs. I stay mostly at the back, with the piles of submitted stories and poems. Heathcote comes down from the Open Head Press office on the floor above, where a publishing partnership with the graphic designer Richard Adams produces a steady stream of anarchist-inspired material. John Sladek, the quiet-footed SF writer, with a mind as many-levelled as a Piranesi prison, has become a lodger in my house; he stays in there most of the time, writing – sometimes, I hope, for us. Ballard comes – but we're unlikely to have dinner out. There's one restaurant opened around the corner from the *Bananas* office in Kensington Park Road, called Duveen's. A visit from *Bananas* staff, however, reports – and later I discover them to be right – a dog's dinner served on a boiling-hot tin plate. There is nothing round here other than Mike's, the caff next door to our office. L'Artiste Assoiffé is too expensive – though Jimmy and I go there once, and sit in the room with the fancy furniture and the parrot that shrieks all day, its call penetrating as far as the stalls, the old clothes and tarnished silver in the market at Westbourne Grove.

NEW YEAR 1975

Michael Moorcock Fights Back

Reception of the first issue of the magazine hasn't been all bad. Admittedly, the small launch party in the gloomily painted dark-green ground-floor room at home was rendered less convivial by the presence of Michael Moorcock, himself the longstanding editor of SF fans' most favoured magazine, *New Worlds* and thus an expert on 'little' magazines. 'At least it's lively,' he pronounced in sepulchral tones, as the sinister-looking paper with the black-and-white grainy picture of the police photo-fit was passed from hand to hand. A pall fell – there's no other way to describe it – and, as ever, it took Ballard's rich, confident pronouncements on the excellence of the venture, to cheer us up – Julian, Rosalind, myself and a gang of helpers and friends.

Outside, on the grim January day, Moorcock's friends, the rock band Hawkwind, hung about with lurchers, looking like actors auditioning for an urban *Robin Hood* . Not for the first time, I wondered why on earth I had wanted to start up a magazine. Haunted by the rubbish bags full of poems at the *Bananas* office, harassed on occasion by the poets themselves – one came up into the office when I was on my own there last week and stood by me at the round table, opening and shutting a black attaché case which contained nothing but a long-bladed kitchen knife – I have started to long for it all to be over even before it's begun.

I suggest to Moorcock and the others that we go up to the Portobello Hotel, for a drink. The brightest spot of glamour in this seedy, decaying area where Polish and German refugees, talking and talking, fill my head with a jumble of tongues, and cabbage leaves from the market lie stinking in the gutters, the Portobello can be counted on to house French lesbian film stars, Americans wearing shades and lonely, enigmatic intellectuals. The rooms are tiny – but Jean Rhys, enjoying her royalties from *Wide Sargasso Sea* after a lifetime of poverty, settles for months at a time in the oval room on the ground floor. Francis Wyndham, who rediscovered her, still alive in the depths of Devon when she had been thought long dead, has taken me to see her there. But the Portobello is up in Stanley Gardens, and no-one feels like hiking it up Ladbroke Grove on a cold, dark evening.

Julian and I go to Bertorelli's in Westbourne Grove and sit over pasta. Then, suddenly, we both see a man who walks past with a shoulder bag, from it poking a copy, just a few hours in the shops, of *Bananas* . We call out to him and he turns, surprised but luckily not annoyed. 'It looks *good*,' he says, but it's impossible to tell whether he's humouring us, or has already read the wonderful contributions of Tom Nairn, Heathcote Williams and J. G. Ballard.

Love and Fear in Notting Hill

I've spent the evening with 'Jim' – as J. G. Ballard,
the visionary creator of drowned worlds, *Vermilion
Sands*, and now at work on a novel about a
motorway desert island, is known to those who wish
to show they are close to him. But perhaps this is a
contradiction in terms. Those who think they know
him really well call him 'Jimmy'. I'm one of those
who can consider themselves close – but all night I
dreamt of brown, muddy water, as if the Yangtze,
the river of his captivity in the Shanghai
concentration camp, surrounds him and anyone in
his vicinity when sleep comes. His tales of the camp
haunt the atmosphere long after he has gone. 'We
pushed the weevils to the side of the plate at first.
But then my father told us to eat them; they
contained all the protein we were likely to get.'

    At dinner, Jimmy has told me of the privations
of his years as a prisoner of war. I begin to realise
how far he is from being a conventional
Englishman, despite the brisk and slightly alarming
air – of family doctor or solicitor – which he
presents to the outside world. This is a man who
was snatched from luxury and put behind barbed
wire for four long years – and the pain suffered then
was compounded when, happily married with three

young children, his wife Mary died suddenly on holiday in Spain. He tells me he thinks the world is going through a death of affect – of feeling, of ability to love, I suppose he means – but of course he refers to himself, and it would be impossible to give a spontaneous hug or caress to the man who writes of atrocities, of light aircraft crashing in overgrown tourist resorts; of despair disguised as revelry.

For all that, Jimmy announced he likes 'neurasthenic women' – what an old-fashioned term! – almost pre-Freudian – do I qualify? I wonder, am I 'neurasthenic' enough for him? Whether I am or not, a few days later at the magazine office in comes L. T., a 'poetess' (another dated term employed by him): small, wiry-haired, hugely enlarged eyes glinting behind horn-rimmed glasses. 'Here!' says L. T. breathlessly, and she hands me an old brown envelope, containing, so I imagine, her latest crop of brilliant imagist poems.

'Can you give it back to Jim Ballard?' A tie, gaudy stripes, recognisably a part of the writer's unsettling wardrobe, is pulled from the recesses of the envelope. Old Jiffy bag fluff fills the already overflowing office. I peer through a grey mist at the poetess, but she has gone.

'I think she's telling us something,' says one of the magazine helpers, after we've gone to the window and looked out at the tiny 'neurasthenic' making her way into the Portobello Road.

The mechanics of running a magazine are hard to
fathom. And for *Bananas*, with what feels like
stone-age equipment – the golfball typewriter is
our one claim to membership of the modern
world – it seems to take an age to get an issue
together.

Columns are measured out on the round
table in the front room; but there are too many
diversions, whether visits from new writers –
Martin Ryle the most promising example so far: tall
and fair, and protective when an 'assistant' art
director, hands trembling from a heavy night in All
Saints Road, suddenly freaks out at my reaction to
his Nazi layout, all coiling Gothic and swastika
lettering – or one of the perennials, such as Mike
Horovitz, glimpsed in Blenheim Crescent, who
stops in his tracks and waves as he gazes thought-
fully up at our psychedelic façade. There never
seems to be time to proofread the articles and
stories, before the paper is laid between boards and
taken to King's Cross, to go Red Star to Diss in
Norfolk. Here I imagine the printers passing as little
comment as possible as they extract the naif art
Julian prefers to illustrate our contents with – or the
Edward Bawden woodcuts, black and surreal when
placed in conjunction with totally unsuitable pieces.
The strange little ads from *Rendezvous* magazine

which our designer dots all through the magazine
must pain and bewilder them, too.

Nevertheless, we do seem to be getting
somewhere at last – and by this I mean the
provinces, where nothing remotely like *Bananas* has
ever been dreamt up or seen. Here is how it went,
today, when I mounted the foul-smelling stairs of 2
Blenheim Crescent and came into the front room –
here, for that matter, is how it goes most days,
unless a major tantrum has removed one or two
people – or the eerie calm of Barry Miles, intent on
his impossible project, that of despatching the
magazine to every campus in America, has emptied
the room entirely.

'The man from W. H. Smith came last night,'
I say.

Silence. I look round the room. Rosalind
Delmar, deep in her research for a feminist history,
leans confidingly over to a young art student, the
handsome José Aguon, who is here to help us in
the late stages of putting together *Bananas* No. 2. A
cover that is worse, if possible, than the photofit of
a female bomber lies on the chipped wooden
surface of the table. On it a woman in a white
gym tunic lies on her back in mid-exercise, leg
raised in the air. The image is far too grainy – it's
an old picture from a gymnastics manual blown
up. Where *does* Julian find them? But it's not
even remotely funny. 'I think I've been working

too hard; I'm going to book a facial,' Rosalind
announces. José nods absently.

My eye sweeps the circular table. If Rosalind is
plump and pink, with a friendly face that can
suddenly fall into furrows of a dreamy
abstractedness, Barry Miles, her other neighbour, is
as quiet and pale as a glass of milk. He never uses
the Barry – I've learnt that. He's just Miles. His face
and hair and eyes are all the same colour and
consistency, as if the archives where he burrows to
dig out the lives of the poets have covered him with
a powdery dust, the pulp of Ginsberg and Burroughs
and Ferlinghetti and Gregory Corso. He is so hip he
gives off no frequency, pulseless he sits with paper
and pen – or the golfball if it's free – and targets the
students of a distant continent. Sometimes I wonder
what they, like the printers in Diss, would think if
they saw our university representative. In his
biscuit suit, beige shirt open at the neck, Miles
could be anything or anyone: would they ever guess
him to be the bibliographer of Beats?

Julian – who looks like a girl in the last
Polaroid photo someone took here: his hair droops
over the collar of his shirt, his lips are full and his
eyes languorous – is apparently half asleep in the
back room, where a daily struggle takes place
between layout and the sorting of poems from the
bin-liners which swallow them. He is interested
really, I know, in the outcome of the visit of the

man from Smith's; but he has no intention of showing it. Anything that smacks of commerce is unbearable to this scion of the Arts and Crafts movement, and however many weird or unexpected images he may come up with for *Bananas*, the soul of his grandfather William Rothenstein lurks deep within him. His father, Michael, is an artist, too, of course. 'I seized him,' I say, trying to make a funny story out of last night's attempt on my part to make a real business out of the magazine. 'I grew so nervous waiting for him that I rushed out of the house and shouted 'Got you!' without thinking. He nearly ran away . . . '

Despite my efforts to amuse, there's still little reaction from the group. I reflect that I'm still nervous anyway, after a man called O'Connor, author of a long-ago bestseller entitled *Memoirs of a Public Baby* came to my house and ran at me, lunging with his cane and shrieking that I was the ugliest woman he had ever seen. (This because I had turned down his son's stories, or one of the reasons at least. I had little desire to admit strange men into the house for a good time after that.)

'I call it patronising,' Rosalind announces, when I've outlined the W. H. Smith proposal – that twenty copies of the magazine be placed in various outlets countrywide, their location not divulged to us.

But I am glad of the plan. It's risible, certainly,

that I would send friends to buy up the paper, if I knew its whereabouts. But who knows? The scheme may work and we will be properly distributed, a magazine as 'real' and accepted as *Encounter* or *Trans-Atlantic Review*.

Meanwhile, it occurs to me that a recent *Time Out* criticism of *Bananas* – that it resembles the out-tray of a literary magazine – has rather hit the nail on the head.

I must bring in the best writers – do magazine editors always think self-importantly like this?

I already have the emotional and intellectual support of J. G. Ballard, who will write for us whatever happens. This exile from old Notting Hill, this Ovid of Suburbia, shall contribute to every issue.

I must, most importantly, find Angela Carter. The basement at Better Books in Charing Cross Road will hold for ever the memory of my first meeting with her extraordinary, scented prose. *Love*, as the book of hers was called, sat on a high shelf, near Borges in his transparent wrapper. I have no idea where I will find her – it's said she went to Japan, then came back.

And the way we live now? The monarchy . . . Tom Nairn, brilliant analyst and forecaster of changes in society that are invisible to most, shall be lured to Notting Hill to write some more.

I leave the room with the round table, and the

summer smell that comes up from the barrows in the market, and walk home. To Marjorie, who helps look after my children. To my room with its blue and white chintz peeling in strips from the walls.

Above, old Mrs Holland treads heavily on broken floorboards as she walks back and forth, making a baked-bean tea. This reminds me that I provided Sladek, who occupies the room next to hers, some weeks ago with a table-top cooker, brand-new, electric, gleaming white, and he has utterly failed to put it together. But then, mad geniuses don't need cookers – especially if they have just published, as Sladek has done, a novel entitled *The Muller-Fokker Effect*. What on earth, I wonder, as I run a bath and contemplate the evening ahead, can *that* possibly be about? Still, its author seems to get along without food or drink. I wonder if Mrs Holland would like to take possession of the cooker in his place . . .

Later, I reflect that we may be accused of being no more than an out-tray of literature – certainly we can't compare with Ian Hamilton's *New Review*, edited from the Pillars of Hercules in Soho – and I accept that each move we make appears to be accompanied by farce or disaster (a huge chunk of the first-floor landing ceiling at 60 Elgin Crescent fell in just as our first major interview, for *The Guardian*, was taking place last week).

But people, if gingerly, are buying *Bananas*. The W. H. Smith plan, of dropping bundles into unnamed stores, has proved positive. We now have distribution on a national scale.

And at last I have tracked down Angela Carter. She came here today to talk about writing for *Bananas*. Somehow the subject was skirted round – and I couldn't get a straight answer, not now anyway.

We sat upstairs, in the room on the first floor, and as we discussed who we hate most amongst contemporary writers she slid to the floor. I soon joined her; we seemed to move, like crabs, towards and away from each other. I felt myself in the presence of a fairy, who might transform the very ordinary room into a Japanese temple. She talked of men in Japan and how clumsy she had felt there . . . her hair streamed or rather floated around her head, white and grey . . . I expected talk of transmogrification, of translation from human to wolf, but 'How much do you think he made from his last book?' says Angela, of Ian McEwan, a fellow writer in Clapham.

Bananas

'*Stand*! What a wonderfully erect title for a
magazine!' The speaker, whose opening words these
are, is a tall man with sharp but kind eyes. He is
James Kirkup, poet and translator, over from Japan
to offer us a blasphemous poem; and as he
brandishes the 'little' magazine of that name (little
in relation to *Bananas*, at least, for *Stand* is squat
and horizontal, not long and Warhol's *Interview* -
shaped). I see that all in the front room at 2
Blenheim Crescent have fixed their gaze on him.

There's something, I can't help concluding as
we gratefully accept Kirkup's offering, about a
magazine such as ours which attracts either support
or instant denigration. Typically, Auberon Waugh
has already attacked us, and *The Guardian* has
praised: generous supporters include Alan Sillitoe
and his wife, the poet Ruth Fainlight; while Charles
Osborne at the Arts Council Literary Panel has –
alas – proved to fall into the Waugh category and
refused to subsidise us.

Equally, we appear to attract if not mixed nuts,
as Californians would term them, then eccentrics of
all shades and hues. Heathcote Williams, of course,
sets out to out-fool Fools – but his most recent play,
The Local Stigmatic, shows such brilliance that to

label him an eccentric would be to disparage his talent. (His occasional visits to me in the evenings at home do, however, merit the description, at least as far as the practical and hard-working Marjorie is concerned: last night, when she put her head round the door, even she blenched at the sight of Heathcote squatting atop the bookcase, grinning, a malign Buddha stripped to the waist and already responsible for the smashed china on the carpet.)

The oddballs who drift into the *Bananas* office are poets, mainly – sometimes girls with closed, inward expressions and bags of incomprehensible stanzas, sometimes young men and women who wish to show their post-'60s art, as much Hockney-fed as the poems are Plath-inspired. Eccentricity, it seems, is the wrong-side-of-the-blanket offspring of real art. When Julian Rothenstein finds a student at the RCA who displays real gifts, there's never a question of 'screwball behaviour' or anything of the sort. Ian Pollock is one of the best examples of the seriouness of the artist, when he illustrates a story for us. Daniel Brand, quiet and pale, brings us his poems ('Nerves 1974– 75' is the one we thought out-standingly good and decided to publish) and he sits and stares at us like an owl. But this gifted seventeen-year-old could never be mistaken for an eccentric.

'My God, you can't even hear the children from here!' It's dark, and what with fireworks going off in the gardens at the back and troupes of Trick-or-Treaters, small Halloween visitants at the door every minute, an emissary from the detested world of 'bourgeois' life has somehow entered the house and penetrated my first-floor sitting-room where I write. Who is it? She has come to offer an invitation to tea to my daughter – but I suspect she just wants a good look round.

'We met with Craig and Anne,' my visitor reminds me. As she mentions the evening at the house of the proprietors and inventors of Ceres, the first health-food emporium in the *quartier*, I see her glance up at the ceiling of my room and the landing outside, as if to reassure herself that there are indeed floors of other rooms and other lodgers – of Mrs Holland who has always been here; John Sladek and his pristine cooker – in the house before you even get to Marjorie and the nursery. 'I'm *so* sorry to barge in,' this mysterious member of the snooping classes announces, before leaving. What did she expect to find here? An opium den? An orgy? Then I think of Heathcote on the bookcase and burst out laughing.

For all my indignation at the accusations of eccentricity directed at the magazine – and at myself, I suppose – the fact remains that there is something upside-down – *la vie à l'envers* as the French so perfectly put it – about life and work in Notting Hill. The days, running a magazine, such as

ours, are all chaos and anarchy. They are given over
– as personified by Heathcote the Jester and Miles
with his quotations from Burroughs or the arrival of
Ballard's manuscripts with holes punched in them
due to the violence of typing – to the Lords of
Misrule. We live in a permanent Saturnalia. Only at
night, when I read or write, or go sometimes into a
world of a hundred Notting Hills, does a sense of
order, of the ability to observe and record, return.
Elaine Feinstein in her translation of Tsvetayeva,
writes: 'In my enormous city it is night'. Here, in
my small but always surprising pocket of London, I
sit at my table and look out at the people passing in
the street. These are the times I like best: the
Notting Hill nights.

Andy Warhol's 15 Minutes

Michael Dempsey asked if he could bring Andy
Warhol to dinner. And now, my basement kitchen in
Elgin Crescent has suddenly filled with men, men
dreary and grey-suited. There are about thirty of
them at the long trestle table, sitting at the bench –
as obviously office-bound and trying to be
'bohemian' as the central figure is unmissable. To
this unappetising board Antonia and Harold,
recently joined, have also come; and, as in a
nightmare, I see that Harold has been placed next to
one of Warhol's cronies, *Penthouse* proprietor Bob

Guccione. How long will Harold be able to take it?

To distract myself from the imminent disaster, I concentrate on Warhol. Wasted, drained of life or interest in the proceedings, he stands out, I decide, not only because he's not wearing a tie (his escorts are from his publishers) but because, like Garbo or Monroe, the very famous on whom he has feasted night and day for so long, he knows himself to be a representative of the Underworld, the nether regions of Fame. True to form, he doesn't speak a word. But sooner or later, something will give – sure enough, Bob Guccione, who is wedged in at the trestle table, asks Harold if he'll let him out. 'I have to call Bianca Jagger,' the porn king says.

Harold is mild but to the point. 'Why do you say you want to call Bianca Jagger?' he says. 'Why don't you just say you want to make a call?'

A few days later, I read a brief account by Warhol of his London visit. The evening at my house is described as 'going to someone's house in Notting Hill, I don't know who'. And I laugh, thinking I've achieved something after all. Fifteen Minutes of Obscurity.

A bad time – Julian has gone away and I've been left to design, lay out, edit etc. the third issue of the magazine.

We are now thought to be 'radical chic' and the Warhol *Interview* format is derided, but people write in more and more and there's a feeling *Bananas* exists, if very precariously, in the world.

I can't fall by the wayside now, I must produce a professional-looking issue of the magazine. Barney Wan, an old friend, a design genius, comes to our office and slowly an issue comes together. Ian McEwan has sent us a story of a man's obsession with a shop mannequin, 'Dead as They Come' – it will lead the contents.

Then there's the extraordinary document that is Harold Pinter's play *Old Times* annotated and written over by Heathcote Williams. Pinter gave us this, and the wild additions and flourishes make a surreal centrepiece for the magazine. Poems by Elaine Feinstein and Jenny Joseph.

A huge red Lissitsky '3' on the cover is as much as I can manage without an art director. Yet *Bananas* No. 3 must be the most promising issue so far. We've put in for an ambitious Arts Council grant: it's the only way we can stay alive, if we get it. Very unlikely: the rather self-conscious irreverence is certain to put off those august personages at 100 Piccadilly.

Round Britain

'It's Tim, calling from the wilds.'

I'm becoming used to the calls that come
through just as I'm at the top of the house giving my
younger daughter a bath. Tim Owens, a friend and
inhabitant of the Westbourne Terrace flat where
Miles sometimes hangs out, is 'found' by him to
help take the magazine to far-flung shops where
W. H. Smith would never penetrate.

I begin to look forward more and more to his
return from these selling ventures, his success due
largely, I suspect, to his great good looks, blazing
eyes and refusal to take no for an answer.

Having Tim on board makes everything run
more smoothly at 2 Blenheim Crescent. As does the
confidence built by the Arts Council awarding us a
grant of £3,000. We still have rent to pay,
contributors who must be remunerated, and all
kinds of financial problems. But we're on the way –
so it seems, at least.

Sylvia Plath and her Relics

The house is one of a terrace, on the fringes of
Camden Town. It's odd to stand on the step outside,
look through the window (no net curtain for the
Keeper of the Plath Flame) and imagine how
different the interior of this house is from the others
on the street. Here may lie the originals of *The
Moon and the Yew Tree*, with all the scorings-out and
the final, triumphant version – here is *Lady Lazarus*
– I admit to feeling a vicarious, journalist's thrill to
have been allowed with so little difficulty into the
shrine where Sylvia's sister-in-law, head priestess,
tends the invaluable relics of a genius.

In fact, the house in Chetwynd Road is more of
a palimpsest of the Plath years of growing fame and
fascination to the public than a place of honour or
remembrance. Once I've been let in (this takes some
time) and led into the 'office' at the back of the
house I see the raw materials of the Private Edition
business: there are volumes of Plath and Hughes
poems in slender tomes with names like Rainbow;
and sheaths of thin paper looking desperately in
need of salvaging, with, as my fevered imagination
supplies, typed poems, half-begun . . . And bills,
some months old, for electricity and gas. There is a
feeling of chaos, of a guardian suffering from the

demands of a delinquent charge. The feeling is soon underscored by Olwyn Hughes's dismissive remarks on the subject of her late sister-in-law – there was clearly no love lost between the brilliant, vulnerable poet and the woman who must now serve her memory and preserve her genius.

Olwyn is tall and must have been strikingly handsome; though, like the little villa with its clear signs of damp and desuetude, she seems in need of a new lease of life. I understand, as she mutters about the 'Women's Libbers' (these in America, mainly, and baying for the blood of the man who murdered their heroine, Sylvia) just how taxing a time Olwyn has had, all these years – thirteen I believe – since Plath was found dead, kneeling by the oven in Fitzroy Road. She has cared for the children – not so much lately, of course, as Ted has remarried. She has cared for the literary estate – but here, as I have said, I feel apprehension at the sheer magnitude of the task she has to mastermind entirely alone. With her long, Spanish-looking face and quick flashes of charm under a harassed exterior, Olwyn makes an odd stand-in for her brother: why doesn't *he* tidy up here? Does he ever come to London?

I'm aware, naturally, that my questions are disingenuous and my real desire is to meet the poet who has now all but retired from the world. Will Olwyn produce him? – she brings him into every

sentence, as a mother would. But the villain of the
Plath poem 'The Rabbit Catcher', it seems, is loth to
travel up from Devon. (I begin to think of him with
the romantic horror Lord Byron must have liked to
inspire in impressionable young women.) And I
think of Sylvia's most obscure and tantalising poem,
of that name; of the cliff where she walked, the
snares set there, the high wind: 'It was a place of
force'. And I remember, as Olwyn murmurs of her
brother's amorous life, 'It's all been such *mayhem*,'
how 'The Rabbit Catcher' goes on, with the line
'How they awaited him, those little deaths!' I feel
suddenly forlorn and depressed, in this house
where the remains of a brilliant mind lie all around.
For gaudy reminiscences of this extraordinary
woman will proliferate over the coming years but
the reality of her death is here, now, with the
crumpled pieces of paper, long-forgotten letters and
bills. I need to leave – but Olwyn catches me by the
arm before I can go.

'You might like to use this.' She thrusts a four-
or five-page manuscript in my face. '"Day of
Success". That's the name of the story. It's all Sylvia
thought about, you know. She wrote it for a
women's magazine. You could get a little artist to do
something to go with it, for your paper.'

Later, at night, I find myself thinking of Ted
Hughes. There's something about Olwyn that is

disturbingly like him – or like I imagine him to be.
Large-boned, with a face that is both powerful and
dreamy – and she makes one listen to what she
says with an intensity (so again I imagine) that
would be better suited to a forceful poet such
as Ted.

I did get the feeling, a slightly uncomfortable
feeling, I confess, that Olwyn is unsure if she
wishes me to meet her brother. There are many
references to the 'terrible time' Ted has undergone,
as if this is what stands in the way of his finding
perfect happiness. Now he is married and faithful to
a beautiful neighbour in Devon. She was a nurse,
and her father is a farmer in Devon, in the patch
where all the 'mayhem' – the marriage to Sylvia and
resulting disaster with the next in line, Assia – took
place. At last, so Elaine told me when I said I was
going round to collect a Plath story from Olwyn, at
last Ted has settled down. He's been married for
seven years.

My feeling of discomfort, I realise, is because,
like so many women who read Plath's famous last
poems in the late '60s, I feel I've lived through a
climate of feminism in which, in colours as crude as
a Punch and Judy show, Sylvia stands for the
martyred female and Hughes for the murderous
male. In spite of – or because of – this over-
simplified positioning of contestants in the ring, a
sizeable part of me wishes to abandon allegiance to

the martyr and saint and throw myself at Ted
Hughes. I am embarrassedly aware that I'm not the
only one to suffer from this suppressed desire. I've
laughed about it with friends: we refer to it as the
Bluebeard or Mr Rochester syndrome, which, also
crudely delineated, consists of a need on the part of
certain women to become involved with a man
known for his terrifying and unacceptable
treatment of members of their sex. Charlotte
Bronte's masterpiece, *Jane Eyre*, is about her
heroine's struggle to escape this compulsion. There
can be no justification for indulging it a hundred
and fifty years later. Yet an extraordinarily large
number of women still do.

I was annoyed with myself today, for finding I
may after all belong to this type of woman – and I
promise myself, however intriguing the news of
Ted's next trip to London and 'You two must meet'
may sound to me, I'll get on with editing the
magazine and finding good writing to put in it. The
allure of the Bluebeards and Mr Rochesters, I
remind myself, lies in their possessing a secret
which the virginal and foolish bride is determined
to seek out. The key to Ted's forbidden door may
have been shown to me by his sister. I don't intend
to make use of it.

The new issue of *Bananas* went to the printers
today. I'm beginning to get a good feeling about

the mix, and I like the way England is seen, as it were, through magnifying glasses, darkly: Tom Nairn on 'The English Enigma' – the un-evolved political climate of this country with its sense of superiority and antiquated constitution; the history of crime in eighteenth-century England, this spurred by poverty and inequality, reviewed by Claud Cockburn; and a trenchant interview with Bernardo Bertolucci by his wife, herself a very un-English film-maker, Clare Peploe.

Claud has come to stay for a few days – he makes everyone here laugh, with his anecdotes of Al Capone or pre-war Vienna, which inevitably end with a gasp, just as his perpetual Woodbine shrivels to ashes and dies.

Marjorie, the blunt-spoken Cornishwoman who helps look after the children, is less than amused by Claud, however. The sheets on the bed in the front room here are held up for inspection daily; and grey, peppered with holes from falling Woodbines, they give her more to complain of than Sladek's furtive visits to the basement bathroom, breakfast cup in hand, as he prepares for his wigwam of hair to take a drenching – or old Mrs Holland's new and alarming habit of leaving a box of household matches on top of the gas cooker upstairs and then absent-mindedly turning it on.

Homage to Salami: Bertolucci and Moravia in
Rome

In Rome – I'm carrying with me *Bananas* No. 4,
with our interview with Bernardo Bertolucci,
'Homage to Salami'. I'm staying with him and Clare
Peploe in a tall, handsome apartment near the
Botanical Gardens. Bernardo, who is fond of teasing
and jokes, nevertheless takes seriously the fact I
have cut so much of the interview, particularly his
encomium on the qualities of a recently dead
friend. Now I feel my cuts *were* in fact unnecessary.
It's not as if *Bananas* is really a newspaper, after all.
We could have added space.

Bernardo takes us – I've come here with Tim
Owens, who distributed early numbers of the
magazine 'in the wilds' – to dark, unposh
restaurants where there isn't a tourist to be seen; to
parties where the talk is all of the murder of Pier
Paolo Pasolini and the loss to Italian literature and
movies caused by his death; and Bernardo and
Clare entertain us, too, at home. Here his father,
Attilio, principal translator of Thomas Hardy into
Italian and highly regarded poet himself, talks
unselfconsciously and happily of everything from
sightseeing to literary magazines. After lunch,
served by a man who looks as if he belongs in
one of Bertolucci's films – serious, slightly
ambiguous – we walk in the palm-tree cool of

the Gardens, a few steps from the building where Bernardo lives.

In the evening we go to see the art historian Milton Gendel in the ex-morgue on the Isola Tiberina, where Antonioni filmed a part of *L'avventura*. I feel excited to find myself a part of this world of Italian movies and intellectual argument, even if I *am* known, by some of Bertolucci's friends, as 'Signora Banana'.

I learnt, I hope, a lesson last night; the lesson being to restrain oneself, if possible, from bringing the subject of self into the conversation when talking with a famous writer – though I must say I found it on this occasion irresistible. Alberto Moravia was the main guest, and Laura Betti the actress, was here; Enzo Siciliano and his wife came too. It is impossible not to be impressed by Moravia: white-haired, with a face so intelligent it seems to be commenting on what it sees and hears without its owner needing to open his mouth. He seemed pleased to be seated next to me, and for the first half of dinner I listened to him and Enzo Siciliano, along with Bernardo's father, the editor of the Italian literary review *Nuova argumente*, as they talked long and passionately. Only about a quarter of the conversation was comprehensible, unfortunately, to me. Then I piped up. Twelve years before, I had published my first novel, *The Colour of Rain*, under a pseudonym, and its publisher, Barley Alison at

Weidenfeld & Nicolson, had submitted it for a prize named the Prix Formentor, held annually in Majorca. My novel was slight and I was surprised at the decision; however, it was mortifying to hear that the head of the judges, Alberto Moravia, had upheld the slim volume and declared it a symptom of British cultural decadence before hurling it into a waste-paper basket (a kind journalist who had been present informed anyone in London who cared to listen of this).

Alberto Moravia showed no pleasure at being reminded at dinner with his good friend Bernardo Bertolucci of his treatment of the British entry to the Prix Formentor; and even less delight on learning his neighbour at dinner was the author of the book so scornfully despatched. Even someone as carried away with themselves, and doubtless with the red wine, as I was that evening, could hardly fail to notice that the evening went downhill after that – Bernardo's teasingly innocent query as to whether Moravia's girlfriend of the time hadn't actually been the winner (hers also a well-known name, and no doubt whatsoever the prize was justly bestowed) giving Moravia occasion first to scowl, and then, when no more than ten minutes had passed, to announce he was tired, and leave.

'What a pity,' Clare says this morning as we sit in the room looking out on trees and the street. And indeed it is. But the phone rings now, with some of the friends I've met since I came here, friends of Bernardo and Clare – and I hear one of them laughing and asking for 'Signora Banana'.

A Bentley in the Bello

Back in London, where the English Enigma of Class presents itself once more. On this occasion, little more embarrassing than this morning's sudden arrival in the street outside the *Bananas* office of a huge, black Bentley, sleek and polished, with a chauffeur at the wheel. (Worse, the chauffeur, whose name is Walters, recognises me as I lean out of the window, alerted by José Aguon, the fine-featured young assistant.) The shop under our first-floor office, known as The Dog Shop, is receiving Walters's patrician glare, following his acknowledgement of my red face and waving hand. The Dog Shop sells Rizlas, along with bric-a-brac of a particularly nauseating kind: it's hard to imagine Walters, let alone his employers, setting foot in there – and I gaze anxiously at the back seat of the Bentley, to ascertain whether Lady A., who has been known to pay lightning visits to the Portobello in search of Indian tablecloths, is a passenger. I'd rather she didn't come up to our floor, where the lavatory is urgently in need of decoration and repair. And I curse myself for being so 'middle-class', as she would describe my attack of

housewifely nerves in the heart of Bohemia. The
fact that this ducal wife of a rich man considers the
Royal Family despicably middle-class too, is not at
present a comfort to me.

It turns out the car has been sent for me, to
take me to lunch at La Pomme d'Amour in Holland
Park Avenue, an expensive restaurant I have visited
only once or twice. How could I have forgotten?
And my mother, just over from Corfu, will be there
too: why am I wearing unflattering jeans and an old
shirt? Worst of all, how can I live down the looks of
frank contempt levelled at me by the denizens of
the upstairs office, where Heathcote, patron of the
Ruff Tuff Squat Agency, has spotted the purring
incongruous presence of the car? Cravenly, I pray
he won't put the Bentley-owners' beautiful house on
his register. 'Class traitor', say the eyes of all who
watch me run out to the coach, wishing it would
turn to a pumpkin and disappear amongst the exotic
fruits a few feet away in the market. Not for the first
time, I remind myself that I am as dominated by
fear of ridicule from all levels of society as it is
possible to be. Seen as posh in this corner of Notting
Hill, I shall be frowned on in Holland Park for my
shabby, insulting attire.

Dinner at the Ruff Tuff Saloon

Someone waved a wand over the dreary dog-
dinner-on-tin-plate restaurant round the corner
from the *Bananas* office and it has become
Monsieur Thompsons a *le patron mange ici* joint
with a palm tree, a feeling of authentic French
provençal with faded ochre walls and pine tables
where you can sit as long as you like. 'Shall we
share a starter?' says Ian Hamilton, poet and
editor of the *New Review*, who has become a friend
despite his kick-off review of *Bananas'* first issue,
as 'a literary magazine like any other, but
raunchy'. Dominique Rocher, proprietor and
maitre d' of Thompsons – as this modest
establishment on the corner of a Portobello Mews
and next to a new dry-cleaner's, soon becomes
known – doesn't mind if all you do is share a
starter. The food is on the whole excellent,
however, even if some of the dishes, like 'skirt of
beef' are weirdly translated, or have clearly been
stewing in translation for some time. The waiters
are so French it's impossible to imagine them
even knowing where England is – and indeed this
corner of Notting Hill would be hard to define in a
travel guide. It's possible to think of it as Albion,
when Mike Horowitz walks past, or as Boadicea's

city, when John Michel, decoder of ancient runes and druidic circles, breezes along the pavement outside. Even more confusing for the garçons of Monsieur Thompson must be the arrival of Heathcote Williams, when he comes to discuss his latest contribution to the magazine. For now, along with the Ruff Tuff Creme Puff agency, with its information on those with second homes, Heathcote claims to have brought off a sort of *Passport to Pimlico* coup by declaring the area just north of the bridge in Ladbroke Grove and the land to the west, a separate zone. He has named it Frestonia. Apart from the understandable annoyance of those who, like Michael Moorcock, have purchased a tower and small attached house in Yorkshire – in order to confront their inner demons and write books – at learning their names are on the Ruff Tuff register, there is a genuine frisson produced by Heathcote's anarchic practices. His hair, which has been described as a 'pubic tornado' and the evangelical look in his eyes seem to suggest the imminent arrival of the Four Horsemen of the Apocalypse. His graffiti – always the same one: 'Valerie Singleton is a Man' – adorn almost every wall of Notting Dale, the low-lying section of this clay-based, jerry-built region. When Heathcote comes to Thompsons, leftovers rise from plates as he grazes and snacks.

Philip Roth's Fitness Regime

Today Philip Roth is sitting at the back of Thompsons in the gloom. Like an ant-eater's, his long snout and bright eyes are trained downwards, on the food he consumes. A book is held up close to the face; Roth most definitely does not wish to be disturbed. I've heard this most inward-looking and remarkable of self-explorers has a room where he writes in Stanley Gardens, up the hill. I know, despite the fact of his apparent great distance from the talk or excitements around him, that every word one says goes into the long, thin head, shaped like a quill with its tufty feathers of black hair, and lies waiting to be inscribed in stone. I had to run to the downstairs Ladies with one writer friend, Caroline Blackwood, when, while discussing her past life, we both suddenly realised that Roth, like a rain cloud on an otherwise fine day, had moved to an adjacent table and was hovering there, apparently absorbed in a book. 'Of *course* he's not her father,' Caroline spluttered – this was the type of conversation we had been engaged in. 'The mussels are bad – I'll be sick – you'll be sick, too . . .' And, before I knew it, we had dived past the monumental figure of Roth – from whose eyes only a tiny gleam of satisfied curiosity escaped – and were desperately trying to throw up in the exiguous downstairs loo. Dominique, patient as ever, had removed the moules marinières (certainly, what looked and tasted like the Thames Estuary lay at the bottom of the bowl) by the time we reappeared. Roth had gone, too.

I'd had an unsuccessful meeting with the author of *Portnoy's Complaint* – perhaps remembering the liver theme in the book made it anyway less than pleasant to find oneself near him at meal times – when, trying to 'bring together' the celebrated American with our own J. G. Ballard, a group of us had eaten at the table with a comfortable banquette, situated by the large plate-glass window of Monsieur Thompson. Roth, on being informed by me that J. G. had written about the US and its corruptions and peculiarities, most recently a volume entitled *Why I Want to Fuck Ronald Reagan*, looked across at Ballard with an assumed air of polite incomprehension. 'So . . . you want to fuck Ronald Reagan?' My thanks for this inauspicious lunch was a glare of fury from the Swiftian Ballard. Roth had effortlessly made him look ridiculous.

The other day, Roth went so far as to invite me to join him in the dark recesses of the restaurant. We talked of nothing much, except Roth's first wife and the novel, *My Life as a Man*, that he'd written about her violent and untimely death. My sympathy was brushed aside; Roth declared himself unperturbed by the outcome of his spouse's tragic accident. 'I'll bring a copy and leave it here for you.' But I'm not sure I want to read anything as cruelly distressing as this book. I have visions of it lingering at Thompsons, inadvertently boiled along with the 'skirt of beef'. And I also think how dead or inanimate wives and girlfriends abound with the (male) writers I meet or know. Those less inclined to realism than Roth seem to enjoy writing about a love affair with a shop mannequin: two stories, one by Ballard and the other by Ian McEwan, have come in to *Bananas*, both concerning artificial women kept by their creepy owners. There doesn't seem to be an equivalent strain in women's writing – there would be an outcry if there was.

After lunch, Roth suggests I 'see' his Stanley Gardens workplace. I go up the hill with him, and then up three floors to the minute flat where he sits over his desk, deep in Nathan Zuckerman, his *alter ego*. There is hardly any space, between desk, armchair and wall, to stand in; but somehow Roth has fitted a rubber mat, green with a swirly pattern, in this tight space, and I find myself – there is nowhere else to go – standing on it. 'For my exercises,' Roth says. A silence falls, and I leave, suddenly aware I don't want to be here at all. Whatever the 'exercises' are, I definitely do not want to be a part of them.

Boiling hot, and a plague of ladybirds in the
communal gardens, where I sit like a prisoner
behind the wire fences that hold off a Carnival
crowd of about half a million people. Fragments of
poems – a Ted Hughes or a Peter Redgrove – float
onto parched grass at my feet. They are joined by
rejects from the slush pile (but then, many see the
whole magazine, I know, as a slush pile; or, as
Hughes reportedly puts it more kindly, 'a rag bag',
and then, Freudianly, 'not like magazines edited by
men, which have a *point* – *Bananas* is open to
anything').

I like Carnival but I hate crowds – and I dislike
the Carnival snobbery which leads the radical-chic
Notting Hill dwellers to boast of acts of violence in
which they have been embroiled on previous bank
holidays. Frank Crichlow, the black community
leader, who is in constant danger of being arrested
on drugs charges by a racist police force – and who
organises Carnival from All Saints Road, the rad
chic's 'front line' dream – is as suspicious of this
war-mongering attitude as any. He wants the young
and old of West Indian descent – the Afro-
Caribbeans as they must now be known – to sell
their wayside jerk chicken and bright-coloured
sweets in peace. He dreads as much as we do the
sudden appearance of a long knife, the crush under

the bridge in Portobello Road, the further threats of a Carnival taken away to a sports arena and there drained of all the vigour the neighbourhood gives it. Yet, looking out beyond the frail, tall fences which divide the elegant houses and the 'White House lawns' that the middle-class residents encourage here, all one can see are dark-green police vans and rows and rows (surely an unnecessary number) of police. It doesn't look good this year, and the intense heat will inflame it all much more.

At least the spirit of Carnival is preferable to the annual parties in the communal gardens. Here, at midsummer and on Guy Fawkes night, the professionals and upwardly mobiles gather and sip wine chilled or mulled while a tame 'Caribbean' band thumps out the same old tune and the white folk dance with their children. There's something depressingly English about the whole performance: a fête in a country garden – only here, the country is as fake as the green wellingtons the Daddies wear and the immigrants who arrived a generation ago are barred unless they happen to be in the band.

I'm back in the house after walking to the end of the road to observe the floats with their great jewelled insects and kings and queens of fancy dress. Each float is followed by a huge crowd and accompanied by ear-splitting sound effects. The funniest part was seeing Professor Hugh Thomas, author of the definitive study of the Spanish civil

war, walking with his wife behind a float. I tried to
wave – Vanessa is an old friend, very short-sighted
but bravely marching to the ultimate crush under
the bridge by Ladbroke Grove tube station – but
neither could see or, obviously, hear me. On
Michael Moorcock's doorstep is a cluster of kids and
SF writers; from time to time a member of the
crowd dodges up the steps and vanishes inside.
Soon Tim and I and my younger daughter, aged
three, will be off to Suffolk, where, I'm told, the
ladybirds are in great evidence on the beaches near
the house we've rented there. The whole world has
become a glistening, enamelled carapace: it's hardly
possible, in the din of Carnival, to imagine peace
and quiet in East Anglia.

Meeting Ted Hughes

The bell rang at one in the morning and for once I was in bed, almost asleep. The voice on the intercom announced an impossible list of visitors, a dream that seemed to have walked in from the crumbling bridges of Moscow, the blighted fields of *Crow* and the ill-starred loves of the man who now lives as a recluse. 'Yevtushenko and Ted Hughes are here,' rasped the voice of my friend Elaine. 'Can we come in for a drink?'

To dress in the dark – a bottle-green woollen dress, square-necked, unflattering, with stripes of an even less favourable horizontal nature – is no easy task when a sound like a foghorn has already begun, on the front steps under my portico, declaiming from Tsvetayeva's 'Poem of the End'. I feel shudders of excitement as I stumble to the mirror, trying to brush my hair in the blackness . . . I don't want to wake Marjorie or the children.

'A historic meeting,' says a tall woman as she steps forward in my kitchen, the poet looming behind her. But he doesn't even smile, as the Russian declaimer and the women gather round us and I don't know if I can help bursting out laughing. We're in a horror movie – but it's real. The loud

Russian chant continues as we stand staring at each other in the gloom.

A whole day has passed, it's getting dark earlier and earlier, and I'm sitting in the first-floor front room, where the windows go all the way down, letting in slabs of night through the dying leaves on the elm outside.

It's odd how meeting someone who's taken up space in the mind – and, whether I admit it or not, Ted Hughes has – is invariably disappointing, like a promised first visit to the theatre for a child: the sickening anticipation, almost dread; the occasion itself blunted by the scale of emotion; the ensuing sense of letdown.

My initial reaction, on shaking hands? A man bowed down under a heavy weight – smaller by far than I had expected (this I now think must have been an optical illusion caused by nerves) – a manner not so much shy as crafty. A *servile* manner: it was as if this famously handsome and arrogant poet was determined to show himself at a disadvantage to the rest of the company – while the Russian strode and crowed in the gloomy basement, Hughes stood with stooped head.

Only later, when we all sat on the floor and Yevtushenko beat out the rhythms of Tsvetayeva's verses, did I glimpse another kind of appearance –

free and straight-limbed, like a rebel leader. Then it disappeared again.

I had a strong sense of an animal in camouflage, using cunning to evade the others' obvious interest in our meeting.

But this deliberate concealment, this ploy of hiding like a king disguised in a beggar's mantle has of course begun to intrigue me. What is he *really* like? I can't help wondering. The rest of the cast assembled in my house in the early hours of the morning fast become *de trop*: I want to be alone with Ted, precisely to restore his true identity to him.

This is ridiculous – or is it the game he always plays, knowing it to be successful?

The Dance

I'm at the trestle table in the basement at No. 60, Elgin Crescent; it's a dinner party – if such is the term, after the cat next door crept in through the extension and ate chunks of the perfect cold salmon laid out ready – yet I'm not even thinking of that, I'm dreaming, I'm miles away.

'There is such a thing as being beleaguered, having too much to do,' announces Jimmy Ballard kindly. He's sitting next to me; my mother is opposite: they must both have noticed my vacant stare for some time now. 'Relax!' Jimmy continues –

it's one of my least favourite commands, from a
man who looks as if he's been wound up so often he
may one day soon spin right off the edge of the
world – 'Take it easy.' (My mother looks uneasy
herself, at these admonishments from a medical
man – Jimmy never lets you forget he trained to be
a doctor.) 'I'll give the party a miss,' Ballard goes on,
correctly divining the reason for my absence-in-all-
but-body at table. 'Have a good time there, look after
yourself.'

It's obvious my swoon-like state is irritating
Jimmy, if no-one else. Have I really become
'fixated' – as he might, just to annoy, describe the
frame of mind I appear to be in – on one more
powerfully mesmerising, even more gifted and
acclaimed, than he? If so, who is the recipient of my
mooning stare, my reveries? How can any other
writer – and it's easy to guess it's bound to be one of
those – draw me like a magnet to his side? How can
any brain match the perfect poetry, the imperial
scorn of the Literary Establishment which fuels the
energy of his symbolist prose, the cacophony of
romance, fear and fatalities that bursts from a
typewriter which pounces so hard on the definite
nature of the end of a sentence that a hole, round
and tiny and perfectly formed, finishes off all major
passages? Who can this paragon of the palely
loitering, this servant of a more dreadful kingdom of
Satan, this Horseman of my Apocalypse, possibly

be? Yet clearly this perfect being exists. Could it be that he is a poet? 'I rate prose over poetry any day,' comes the declaration, made to my startled mother. '*Anyone* can write poetry.'

But the famous dismissive phrases don't this evening reach their target and I sit on, dead to the world. Further down the table are John Sladek, a couple of *Bananas* helpers and, at the end of the table, the gaunt figure of Claud Cockburn, paying one of his visits from Ireland to these shores. They're discussing my idea – a bad one, I can tell already – of printing a short story I found in a long-out-of-print paperback up in the second-hand bookshop at Notting Hill Gate.

'It wouldn't be news now, would it?' says Claud, trying to catch my eye, perhaps noting its glazed condition. His fingers, long and stained as old mah-jong pieces, fan out, adding to the bizarre impression one gets of Claud as a Northern Chinese. He was born in China, and I've teased him in the past with my theory of 'topogenesis', whereby the place of birth affects appearance and character. 'I mean, a short story by Napoleon isn't a scoop,' Claud goes on, further diminishing what sounds more and more like the worst idea I've entertained for some time. 'Now if it was by Hitler . . . '

I wake up a bit at this; Sladek giggles into his silky black beard, and several of us agree a story by Hitler would be just as unappealing as one by

Bonaparte. The salmon makes the rounds, with a huge salad in a Portuguese bowl that has travelled with me from Chelsea, and I walk, returned to my trance, to the wooden island in the kitchen the last owners built there and I never got round to pulling down. Here is the cheese, looking much as if my dog has given it the same treatment as the neighbour's cat gave the fish. I carry it over, as the Hitler's story argument goes on. 'But who says he ever wrote one?' I manage to put in, feebly.

The meal seems interminable. I may be 'miles away', but in fact it's no more than half a mile, as the crow flies, I think to myself – and then see I mean as Crow flies, the obscene, unrepentant bird of Ted Hughes's poetry. Crow will be at the party. It is my fault – this, for some obscure reason, is how I see the possible appearance, in the Powis Terrace flat belonging to friends, of the poet who has been vilified for years and has lived for the last seven with his second wife in the depths of the West Country. Crow never comes to London, Crow doesn't go to parties. Yet, when I told a mutual friend a few days back that there is to be a party in a glamorous flat – Hockney's old flat, carved from two houses just a few streets east of here – she laughed and said she'd tell Ted: 'You never know, he might like to come.' My distracted state can be put down solely to the fact I'm pretty sure he will.

Some of us go to the party, some don't. The night is fine and dry – but it's cold, and I tremble with impatience as coats are found and then lost in the hall, and Claud decides to come when he'd said he didn't want to. By now Ballard has shot off down the motorway he hymns, in the dark-green station wagon that adds to the image of solid bourgeois, a good father and householder at the wheel (and indeed he is both of these things), a man leading a life of respectability while underneath simmers the surrealist soul of a René Magritte. Sladek, soft-footed in his moccasins, has mounted to the abstruse calculations, both literary and figure-dominated, which take up his waking and sleeping hours. My mother goes back to the flat she has rented on a brief visit from Greece. With Claud, who folds up like an anglepoise lamp when required to enter a car, we drive the couple of hundred yards to the ex-Hockney flat. I feel the magnetic pull of the one person I want to see, and I know I have no idea what I shall do if he is there and even less of an inkling if he is not. I am an arrow, and as soon as I've pressed the bell and entered the grubby hall and gone up the unprepossessing stairs – neither giving any indication of the gorgeous flat above – I can feel my feathered tip as it homes in, even see people dodge as, manically, I make my way through a sunken room, a sitting-room, a long dining-room where some still sit drinking and talking, to a room that is dark and half empty, a room where music plays loud and irresponsible as I.

Ted Hughes is sitting at a round table with a glass in front of him, and another man – I don't even see him – at his side. There is something sprawling, almost disrespectful, in his way of taking up space here – but I discover, as I go straight up to him, that there's a reason for the stretched-out legs and almost horizontal pose. However, I'm treated to a laughing face, a face very much like a satyr's, in the red and black light in this room where a few people dance and the corners lie empty, as if waiting for the night to fill them with shadows of people kissing and clinging together. The laugh is followed by an introduction (I didn't hear it) and the male companion slinks off. Even as early as this I'm aware of the presence of other women: one looks in, pops her head round the door, another strains to look at the man by the table as she dances face to face with someone else.

'I was telling . . . ' Ted waves to the stranger he had been talking to. 'I swapped fairy tales, you could say. Do you know the one about the man who went in search of a princess?'

'Come and dance,' I say. My voice sounds as if I've left it behind, in the basement with the picked-to-pieces salmon and – probably – the prowling cat from next door with its mysterious way of getting in.

'I can't dance,' Ted says.

'*Dance*,' I say. I'm aware of the woman who has popped her head round the door, beginning to walk towards us across the rugless floor.

'Listen to the story instead. The man reaches a tall tower. He enters. The princess is there, but there is one condition that has to be fulfilled, if she is to marry a suitor . . . '

I see the woman – youngish, dark-haired, who must have been brought along with Ted to the party, for she approaches with the look of a housewife in a market, about to snaffle the ripest plums. She stops and stands, arms akimbo.

'The man is in the dungeon of the tower,' Hughes continues imperturbably. 'He looks up. Then he feels it. The Princess shits – from a very great height . . . '

The young woman steps up close. I put out my hand and Ted grabs it. We dance – wildly from the very start, too wildly to go on for long – immoderately, incautiously – foolishly, I see, for the room becomes full of people, as if our dance has sounded a clarion call to wake the dead, the too-polite, all those who have forgotten the terrible energy of Life.

'You're a fantastic woman,' Ted shouts over the music.

Then it all ends as suddenly as it started. The dance is over, the young woman has disappeared

but another friend comes in, to remonstrate with
the poet for 'hurting your bad back' – and, in a party
of four or five which had been invisible before, they
have gone.

Claud is telling his anecdotes to the stranger
who had 'swapped' fairy tales, his wheezing laugh
sounds out in the dining-room with its army of
drained glasses.

The colours, the blues and reds I had seen all
round me, lose their force, even their reality. I'm
awake – hot still from the wild dancing, feeling the
first cold of the winter evening as I step out into
the deserted Notting Hill street. It's time to go
home.

Now it's evening again. The day went by in a blur;
marked mainly by my impatience: never has the
golfball typewriter seemed slower, or the day more
'through the looking-glass'; even the new poems
seem madder – and sadder – than usual. I'm glad to
be back at home and this time I draw the curtains
against the dark. In the faint light from the 1920s
French lamps found in Westbourne Grove, the
expanse of curtained window gleams yellow and
pink, the design abstract and far from rosy or
chintz.

But I'm not sure I really feel safe. I promised
myself I wouldn't give time to thinking about last
night – but of course I have, and my main

conclusion is one I hadn't expected to come to.
Passivity is a strong male weapon of seduction.

My friend Dinny, who is skilled at looking at
human behaviour from new and sometimes
alarming angles, announces that my
determination to sweep Ted onto the dance floor –
and my refusal to be dismayed by the horde of
female carers and admirers around him – came
from Ted himself. 'He probably doesn't even have
a bad back,' Dinny laughed. 'He forced you to
declare your interest.'

Now, a day later, I can't help agreeing with her.
I feel, too, a fool to have made so evident an interest
I hardly knew I had. The thought of the 'other
women' – whoever they may be – and their quiet
satisfaction at my departure, makes my cheeks
flame with irritation. Next time I'll show nothing –
but why do I assume there will be a next time, and
who cares if there is one, or not?

Part of me, though, knows the timing in this
affair has been carefully worked out. Today a
person from Arvon, the centre for teaching creative
writing in Devon that Ted founded, rang to invite
me down there as a tutor. Elaine Feinstein will be
the other teacher of poetry and prose. I'm flattered,
naturally: *Hotel de Dream*, my third and latest
novel, must be considered good enough for me to
assume the role of instructor to would-be writers. I
glow with a sense of self-importance – but that

other part of me wonders, too, whether this isn't a set-up: for the future, for the coming together of myself and Ted which now appears to be written in the stars.

Although the magazine doesn't appear to suffer from the frenzy of deadlines, I've been trying to meet people who will write long pieces for us and who will come in on time. I hope Martin Seymour-Smith will be one of these: I'd admired him for his encyclopaedias in which writers from everywhere in the world are introduced and brilliantly discussed, and felt nervous of meeting him. He hates the 'values' in much of British writing today. After finding, amongst many other masterpieces, Knut Hamsun's *Hunger* and Sadegh Hedayat's *The Blind Owl* through his pages, I have nothing but gratitude towards Seymour-Smith. Or do I call him Martin? He came for a drink last night – and seems professional and rather drunk and out of control at the same time. We sat up too late, talking – but the outcome will be his long piece on today's literary establishment, 'A Climate of Warm Indifference'. It will be the most important contribution in *Bananas* No. 6.

Poems very good too, by Libby Houston and the magicians of Cornwall, Peter Redgrove and Penelope Shuttle.

I'm in a pigsty – literally – in the converted Devon longhouse where the Arvon Foundation, Ted Hughes's school for aspiring writers, is based. Elaine and I will be tutors, over a long weekend. Students, paying but subsidised by Arvon, will be expected to do some of the cooking and then write their own efforts in scattered barns, dovecotes and outhouses while Elaine and I do nothing much – or so it appears – in the pigsty until the stories and poems are ready to be seen.

Even as we left London I had a feeling this wasn't going to be an easy, lazy weekend. Both Olwyn and Elaine seemed certain that I should accept this invitation to teach at Arvon; and when I asked, rather nervously, what the 'teaching' would involve, Olwyn brushed away my question with an assurance that I would be expected only to read from my novel *Hotel de Dream* and that 'Ted will look in, he usually does – ask him to take you to Court Green' (his house a few miles off at North Tawton, famously where he spent the bulk of his married years with Sylvia). Elaine, who has done this before, is clearer when I enquire what my duties will be. Yet by the time we're driving in a small van packed with eager students along the high hedgerow lanes of Devon, I have come to the conclusion a possible romance between myself and

Ted Hughes is a part of an unwritten curriculum –
devised entirely by myself, I confess. Ted and I
have met only twice, and without the dramatic
consequences that I appear to expect. Such is the
power, I try to tell myself, of the female
imagination. I begin to wish I hadn't come to
Devon.

This is an exaggerated way to think, of course,
and I concentrate on the pleasant realisation, as we
drive along, that Ted obviously does care very much
indeed about giving kids a chance to be helped in
their writing. These kids are grown-up, it's true –
but I remember all his poetry competitions for
children, the efforts made to inspire and release the
demon of expression so often crushed in the
educational system – and I think admiringly of him.
That we're going deep into the country where
Sylvia's famous poems, the happy ones like 'The
Bee Keeper', the cries of despair at the moon
'dragging her blacks' which her husband's infidelity
provoked, doesn't seem as pressing a matter today
as I'd expected it to be. Sylvia represents death. Ted,
by showing the young how to set down their songs,
is the spirit of life. I see Elaine looking at me to
catch my reaction as the van turns up a pitted drive
to the longhouse, Ted's kingdom where his
wonderful voice and extraordinary looks reign as in
a fairy story, in bright, crude colours to which one
can hardly fail to respond.

On the way down to Sheepwash (even the name has a fairy-tale quality) I've been thinking of people who have a past – people in early middle age – who run away together.

I think, inevitably, of Caroline and 'Cal' – as Robert Lowell is known – of the stories she tells me of the times he goes mad, starting with a dreadful pain in his back, and of the full responsibility of their domestic life falling on her shoulders. The time their swimming-pool at the house they rented in Kent was found to contain a horse, alive and kicking, and the effect on Lowell, at that time in his mania at the 'touch and go' stage, so a surreal scene like this is liable to set him off. The accidents which befall the children and the home – for neither of the parent figures is really capable of handling everyday life.

I come back to the present as the van scrunches to a halt and the female half of the two resident housekeepers welcomes us to the longhouse. The young woman, bright-eyed, pointy-chinned, takes, as I see, an instant dislike to me. She shows us, the tutors, to the pigsty and cannot resist informing me I remind her of a 'do-gooding aunt' of hers. Why does she say that? I wonder . . . But some underground knowledge of women suggests our Arvon hostess tries to put me in my place, make me seem old, in order to remove competition when the overlord, the poet of *Crow* and *Lupercal*, pays his seigneurial visit to the place.

Students settle and then are driven to Okehampton to buy food for the interminable stew which will provide the staple fare for the weekend. Elaine and I dawdle in the October-bright grounds of the ancient thatched building. I feel the first tremors of apprehension: does she see me look out for a visit already? Why do I find myself asking so frequently about the present marriage of the Bard? (But I can't help shrugging bad-temperedly when Elaine says of his wife, 'Very pretty. What? No, dark – and a calming presence; she's the only one Ted's stayed with, after all.') All this – but why? – is provoking to me.

We get through the awkward mess of an evening more inclined to remove my faith in natural talent than otherwise. The students are keen to gossip, and all are looking forward to Ted Hughes and his weekend guest (Yevgeny Yevtushenko again, it is said: Elaine, translator of Marina Tsvetayeva, knows the Russian poets and grows in stature in the eyes of the students). There is little mention of Ted (already, I'm calling him Ted, like a groupie, I think wretchedly). I go as far as to wish he will come alone, without the wife with the beauty and the calming presence. Even thinking of his young wife makes me feel, precisely, like an aunt, though perhaps not a particularly do-gooding one.

We are all at a long trestle table in the longhouse when he comes – and I'm unable to resist thinking that we could be at one of those medieval reconstruction weekends the tourists love to attend at moated manor houses up and down the land. The Arvon resident housekeeper, sure enough, wears her most winsome smile when she walks forward to greet the royal party (Ted's wife is indeed here, and looks the already outlined image of sweetness as well as dark loveliness). Yevgeny is there – he darts me a look of dislike and disapproval not far from the Arvon lady's. After we've all risen and shuffled the chairs about, a silence falls as the students await a pronouncement on the meaning of art from Ted, who has, to my consternation and delight, placed himself next to me.

My admiration has grown all evening, for this man whose tragedies mark him as a villain to many – though many equally I know, defend him in the thorny question of his treatment of Sylvia and his leaving her for another (a dark beauty) and their subsequent love affair, all this outlined by friends over previous weeks. I admire the way he doesn't waffle or give meaningless hope to the students. I see their faces relax in relief: perhaps, if they're true to themselves, they will write exactly as they want to and should. Ted turns to me, when he's spoken a few friendly words. He invites us over to Court Green tomorrow. The Arvon lady says in clipped tones that we're needed here – but (and after all he holds all the cards) she finds herself persuaded by the distinguished visitor to let us go over for lunch. Stories and other submissions will be ready for perusal by the time we return.

I stumble somehow through my reading. Elaine is more successful with her poems, which have a wonderful, light-and-dark quality and clearly inspire the guests. I go to bed in the pigsty, noting that one girl, Kate, who has already pressed half a story into my hands, has definite talent. I decide to keep an eye on her – and possibly, if the story really holds, to suggest we publish it in the magazine.

'I could make you a table, if you like.' We are at Court Green, outside in the courtyard before going in – a stash of wide wooden beams are propped against a workroom door and we're all standing there, as if afraid to go in: Yevgeny has been ribbing Ted (he came to fetch me in his car from Arvon: we've just raced through the Devon lanes to get here) on his keenness to bring a tutor to his house. Carol, Ted's wife, Elaine and I also stand by the door to Court Green. It's as if the great oak beams are barring our way in – though Ted would clearly give anything to move away from Yevgeny's tactless teasing on the subject of amorous journeys and the like. I can't help wondering if Russian men can really act this way and go unpunished by wives or girlfriends . . . but, once we're inside and Yevtushenko, after asking my age (I tell him: thirty-eight) launches into a long story about a love affair he had enjoyed as an adolescent with his schoolteacher, a woman of about my age, I see they can and do.

'A work-table,' Ted insists, running his hand along the grain of the wood. Slavishly, I follow suit; but an uncomfortable sensation possesses me, one that dodges round the strangeness of being offered a work-table, several weeks' labour no doubt, when I don't know the offerer, nor he me. I have to come out from my hiding-place in my thoughts and accept – though of course this is hardly possible – that I'm being turned into someone else by means of this table, a table for a writer which will tip me into the shoes of the woman who was once his wife. All this in front of an audience – including his present wife – but the worst part of my strange sensation is that I feel almost at once responsible for foolishly exaggerated suppositions: why shouldn't the poor man simply want to make a table, and be looking for any writer to give it to, so strong is his desire to start planing this beautiful wood? (Somehow, though, the argument doesn't wash. It leaves me with a strong dislike of myself, for having entered the melodramatic world I had promised I would have nothing to do with, before embarking on my visit here.)

Court Green inside is as far removed in character and atmosphere from the house the world imagines as Sylvia's house as Ted's wife's calm presence is from the histrionic accounts of Ted's life with women before he married her. The house is comfortable, almost refined in its cleanliness and soft colours. Polished table and chairs gleam, the oven holds a careful meal for these unexpected visitors, and we sit politely, nursing glasses and eating nuts as the food warms. It's like finding a lion in a well-mannered small country hotel, I reflect, looking at Ted (who has once more placed himself next to me). There may be a roar, suddenly, or a crash as a casual swipe of paw brings dainty crockery to the ground. But there is none of this – a desultory conversation, nothing more. When we've eaten, the inevitable phone call comes from Arvon and the woman the supervisor probably no longer sees as a do-gooding aunt is recalled, along with her co-tutor, to her duties at the longhouse. We finish our coffee and file out – a taxi has been called to take us to Sheepwash, as Ted and Yevgeny want some time together this afternoon.

As I leave I look back at the doorway where Ted stands alone, waving – and at the tall, pale shafts of wood, like up-ended coffins at the entrance to the carpentry store. Already too many images of death crowd in on me. Along with them, I hear

Elaine's voice as she asks me if I think I am likely to see Ted again, one day.

'I've no idea,' I say. But somehow I think it likely that I will.

In the train from Exeter on my own for the first time in four days, I began to realise how strong Ted's magnetism can be. I'm holding a slim volume of his translations of the Hungarian poet János Pilinszky – he gave me the book in the pub at Hatherleigh where we all stopped for a drink – and his inscription to me (it's the first time I've seen his black, barbed-wire handwriting) made me feel the words burn into me. Ted writes so the sparks fly off the anvil. I stare in the October darkness into the night as Devon and Somerset flee under the wheels; but what I really see is the reflection of my own face: apprehensive, bug-eyed with the day I've just spent. In the rattle and creak of the coaches and the whine of the engine I hear only one phrase, over and over: 'If you like, I'll make you a table.'

I have to stop myself from thinking he might; and I might sit and write at it one day.

A Bananas *Garden Party:*
J. G. Ballard, Angus Wilson and the Queen of Fast Food

If only the magazine had enough money to stay afloat, I'd be really happy with the way things are going. It seems that both Angela Carter and Jimmy Ballard have got into their stride, writing for *Bananas*: Angela in the current issue with 'The Company of Wolves', which is quite the best thing she has done, and Jimmy coming free at last of the constraints on his Shanghai childhood and prison-camp internment, with 'The Dead Time' – upsetting and terrifying but recognisably the landscape of his purposely forgotten corpse-strewn youth.

Both came to dinner last night – not dinner really, but a garden party with food by Luisa, who likes to come and pile on a plate chicken drum-sticks and pizzas and what she refers to as 'fing' food: 'You slowing up, Emma. Used to move house and give party the same night. Now only a party sometimes,' and I always rise to her bait, mainly I think because it gives her such pleasure when I do.

Luisa has become a famous figure since setting up on her own as provider of dinners for the art and smart, such as George Orwell's widow, Sonia. There are eager demands for her phone number from people who have just eaten her spinach soufflé or sweet–sour duck and red cabbage, all achieved in what seems like less than ten minutes. Coming in from Battersea in a mini-cab or by bus, Luisa attracts a lot of attention, by virtue of her pretty face, her adipose body, and the stinging, sarcastic wit that has come with her all the way from Positano. She is married to the man who used to drive and look after my father: her husband John McCubbin is much older than she, and, like my father, retired; but Luisa still likes to send up the old-retainer relationship when she gets the chance.

The 'garden parties' sound like something at Buckingham Palace but consist here of people walking out of the basement kitchen into the small back garden and thence, if it fills up, into the communals – pronounced, round here 'commUNals', just as Elgin is said with a soft g. A soft-g Elgin-pronouncer can be counted on to be a native of the area and not an incomer, who says the word as it is spoken in the North of Scotland, with a hard g – this standing for grand Highlands connections and a knowledge of the town selling tartan and cashmeres to the rich. Luisa, who has her own inimitable language, looks on my writing activities and (doubtless) the editing of a literary magazine as 'Keep you occupy' and nothing more. She also likes to shout her comments to guests as they eat or talk, and last night was no exception, her

brisk interruptions to a first conversation between
Angus Wilson and J. G. Ballard punctuating what
they had possibly hoped would break the literary
ice and form the basis of a friendship.

Angus Wilson to Ballard: Who, in your opinion, is
the most outstanding science fiction writer at
present?

Luisa (coming over with pizzas) to Ballard: You put
on weight since last time I see you. Go on,
take more.

Ballard to Angus: Arthur C. Clarke in my opinion. A
remarkable writer.

Luisa to Angus: Didn't I see you at Anne's – you no
a friend of Anne? I see you talking to Polly
there.

Angus to Ballard: Ah yes, Arthur C. Clarke. I think I
was the one who put him on the map. (To
Luisa): How delicious; but I won't, thank you.

Luisa to Ballard: Why you no married?

Ballard to Angus: Of course Clarke isn't really any
good at all . . .

The old *Bananas* standbys were all here – Julian
Rothenstein and the art student, Hiang Kee, he now
lives with; Peter Wollen, who has written an
enigmatic story for the magazine entitled
'Friendship's Death' (he is revered as author of *Signs
and Meaning in the Cinema* and a group of young
cinéastes clusters around him.) Laura Mulvey,

married to Peter, who is equally known for her work
on women and film. Angela – well, Angela really
needs a few words to herself, but words are, it
seems, what Angela both controls magically in her
writing and finds hard to enunciate or force from
her lips. I wander outside, where the trees are
newly in leaf and people are holding their *Bananas*
No. 7 as if it had just floated down from above:
Angela, I think secretly delighted with her
'Company of Wolves', comes over to kiss me and
non-communicate her feelings. In fact, Angela's
fascination is so great that it doesn't matter how
long one has to wait for the tentatively begun
sentence – this broken into by the chisel of high
laughter, or the power-drill of an indrawn breath, for
she is as amused as any by the kaleidoscope of
thought processes which interrupt the
consummation of her sentence. I imagine whole
libraries and encyclopaedias of alternative
meanings and parentheses lining up within
Angela as she embarks bravely on speech. In the
end, she has said only that she likes the way her
story looks. But all the other possibilities, like
bubbles blown high into the atmosphere,
are there.

Angela's latest book, *The Infernal Desire
Machine of Dr Hoffman*, came out this year and she
is beginning to be known as the importer of magic
realism into this country, so long mired in novels

about class or north–south divisions. Angus Wilson, who admires her writing, comes over to us. And I think it's sad that Angus, who looks very old – but then, he tells us, he always has – is suffering from the attacks on his own recent novel, *As if by Magic*. The attacks come from those he describes as the 'spiteful babies' – in particular Martin Amis and Auberon Waugh – and Angus feels ancient and despised. He does so much for younger writers and has written so many extraordinary novels and short stories that it seems ridiculous he should mind so much. His friend Tony Garratt, the cleverest and kindest of men, tries to take Angus's mind off these shameful barbs.

It grows dark. Someone has brought along a clutch of poets (our contingent comprises Elaine Feinstein, Ruth Fainlight and James Greene, translator from the Russian), and someone says how tall trees in a London garden are beautiful. They are – but before I can float away in poetic appreciation Luisa has announced from the back kitchen door that 'I go now'. This will mean a mini-cab out at front and a bunch of Italian relatives and friends, to go back to Battersea. We're putting a page of 'Luisa's Literary Dinners' in the magazine, with recipes (she's such a name-dropper after an evening at Mrs Orwell's) with names like Haddock Naipaul and Oeufs Lacan.

Ted Hughes and his Past

Left the house early – always a sign of nerves, especially if the meeting-place is practically on top of where one lives – and had to go back in several times, another sign of appalling jitters, to fetch scarf, change coat, etc. I see the stump of the elm they came and cut down while I was lying in bed one afternoon with a hangover has a fresh, glaring colour to it today: why is it that anything to do with Ted Hughes becomes immediately symbolic (my life about to be cut off?) and scarifyingly nasty (colour of amputated wood the fresh brown-red of the injured lambs he writes of with such loving pain)? Why can't I see myself quite 'normally', as an editor going to ask a famous poet to contribute to her magazine? But the question is too far-fetched to bear repeating. I can't, as my hurrying steps and breathless gasping run proclaim, be anything other than an approaching victim – 'a *neurasthenic*', as Ballard pronounces when he comes across a suitable candidate for the sacrifice. I can no longer envisage myself as anything other than this. Embarrassingly obviously, a willing sacrifice to say the least.

Elgin Crescent, partly gentrified – one professional owner collects Roman coins, I see him poring over them in his study as I run by, another,

an avid Gardens Committee type, stares from her
window at me already disapproving of a crime she
can barely envisage – has never seemed more pre-
tentious, with its accumulating number of Venetian
colours on the façades and carefully accentuated
stucco. It flashes through my mind as I race past
Thomas Pakenham's mansion (an aura of historical
tomes seems to emanate from the ground floor
though the long-faced bibliomane isn't himself on
show) that this world of 'upwardly mobile' people
appears to be the antithesis of everything Hughes
loves and stands for. Passions are muted here, or so
tied up with snobberies they have gone into hiding.
A picture of the father-of-three and eminent
businessman who dresses up as a satin-gowned,
high-heeled woman each year at the garden party
comes to mind, as I run across Rosmead Road and
into the stretch of smaller houses – 'the seedy end',
as one resident is pleased to term it, of Elgin
Crescent. I hear in memory the patter of applause –
inevitably, our annual pantomime dame is rewarded
with first prize for his travesty. In the evening he will
dance, immaculate in a tuxedo, to the Caribbean band
imported from the 'rough' streets north of Portobello.

None of this can I confide to my coming lunch
partner with any chance of being found amusing or
perceptive on the subject of local customs and *mores*.
I might as well, I tell myself with a smile as I dash
over the crossing that separates Elgin Crescent from

Clarendon Road, tell my stories of class rivalries and
self-improvement to a personage from the antique
world – a member of the House of Atreus, perhaps,
or the guardian of a shrine to Minos, the bull-god.
Then come self-consciousness and embarrassment
again. I've met Ted only casually and the suggestion
of lunch was, I'm sure, totally innocent. He's happily
married and lives in Devon, farming, for heaven's
sake. He may have a poem for the paper – didn't he
say as much? Turning down from Clarendon Road
into the quaint little hill that is Clarendon Cross, I
try to rid myself of the persistent (and corny) images
the Bard inspires. Many of these are from the animal
kingdom, and are annoyingly strong: wolf, bull – and
– stallion or lion. Nearly all are closely connected
with danger, sex and death. Hughes may be dangerous; but the threat he poses is harder to define than,
say, Lord Byron's must have been. One thing is
certain – and I try, equally, to rid myself of my
dreadful propensity to make literary comparisons as
I reach the bottom of the hill and stand, trying to
catch my breath – one thing is definitely the case. As
a hero pined for by women (in England, at any rate;
in America Hughes is still considered the killer of
Sylvia Plath), he represents an England as far from
the little piece of ivory of Jane Austen as one can
get. It is impossible to imagine him striding across
the lawns of a stately home in Hampshire or Kent.
Mr Darcy he most definitely is not.

Horror. I'm gazing straight at the plate-glass windows of Julie's Bar and yet something tells me to look to the left, to the stretch of Portland Road as it comes up from Holland Park. There he is. He walks along – worse, he sees me but he doesn't look pleased – and I know, in the secret code, a code of instinctive behaviour, of animal recognisance, that I have somehow come at the wrong time and he isn't meant to be seen there, vulnerable, strolling across the veld (as my over-heated imagination sees it). I should have come in, to find him at a table – the best table, of course – and, once more, this appears contrived, for, again like the beast which does not look its quarry in the eye, the man with whom I thought I was about to exchange a polite lunchtime greeting has in the wink of an eye disappeared.

To walk through Julie's Bar, the heavy velvet of the banquettes, the embroidered cushions and the long crêpe-de-Chine skirts of the posh-hippy girls, some serving, others drinking and eating, is like trying to penetrate a jungle where every obstacle brings a clumsy near-fall and smiles and bright eyes flash from the artificial greenery. Upstairs the room is long and as cluttered as an auctioneer's store-room, with elaborate furniture and people lying right back in chaises longues with plates balanced near them – am I to lie like that? I wonder – upstairs is indeed where I find him, at last. The table, at just the right angle to the window, is high

and important and serves as a kind of shield
between us, when I come to stand awkwardly by
the bright circular mahogany. Hughes has ensured
there is only one object on the table – he waves
away knives and forks and glasses as I approach.
Gaudete, says the bright lettering on the volume,
smart and funky in its new Faber hardback jacket.
Hughes's just-published epic poem is on Satan in
the rural England of which Miss Austen never
dreamt. It is already open at the title page. I see the
words, upside-down and as if from a long way away.

> Emma
>> love
>>> Ted

says the deceptively mild script, a beautiful hand, in
thick black ink from a fountain pen, still poised. 'I
was out of cartridges,' Hughes says with an equal
mildness. Thus he admits to having seen me at the
junction of Clarendon Cross and Portland Road, and
by default owns to the impossibly quick capture of
table, the adoption of the book-signing pose, and all.
Was the man transported up here by a magic
carpet? The longing, already loving look in the eyes
of the dark-tressed waitress who comes with wine
and a basket of bread to the table commandeered on
the first floor of Julie's Bar, should, as I see now,
have answered my question forthwith. Where this
man goes, his own brand of magic goes with him.

Close up, Ted Hughes is magnificent. His face, like an Easter Island statue, seems to dominate the surrounding landscape: anger, certainty and pride give an unchanging air to the features; but, as if unwilled by himself, a smile, thin and nervous, plays around the lips. Can he be as eaten with fear as I am at the prospect of this encounter? Or is this the smile on the face of the tiger? As before, animal similes come only too easily to mind. Or is the smile voluntary, an assurance that a wolfish mouth doesn't necessarily mean it won't be *fun* being eaten? I am against my better judgement reminded of Angela (Carter) and her passion for wolves, for hairy men who will suffocate her with their embrace. Has Angela . . . I wonder . . . and it comes to me that she said a few months back when I spoke of Hughes's sudden nocturnal visit to my basement kitchen that there had been 'something' between them. 'But an old fox doesn't need to learn new tricks,' Angela said, with a great shrieking bellow of laughter and her eyes gleamed from under her Red Riding Hood's Grandma coating of white hair. As I think of it, as Ted fingers the salt and pepper pots and moves his (only fairly elegant) pen from one side of the table to another, I feel a retrospective, utterly pointless pang of jealousy. Does this effigy, this god of masculine beauty, of unthinking cruelty, like to eat women artists? Is that all I am to him?

I am hardly seated at the table before Hughes is into a litany of his love disasters, and I hear them with increasing astonishment. The girl before last, who burnt his house in the North, but it was so damp that only the centres of the rooms ignited, his papers, all his poems 'and the pots and pans I made her use' – here a mighty chuckle. The one who reported him to the police as a Yorkshire Ripper, a motorway madman, so he was arrested on a daily basis as he came and went from his home. The time he was returning from Devon to the flat of a girl he lived with and ran over a hare on the way – the voice drops, for a moment the eyes, greeny-grey, look as frighteningly intense as a stage hypnotist's would, to a child. 'And the hare was running again, after it died, and the future was told from the entrails in the girl's kitchen there.' I shudder, I feel myself exhibiting these juvenile symptoms – why am I being told all this? Is this what Bluebeard did, when he brought a new victim to the castle, before showing her the key to the Bloody Chamber? Is this his message for me – that I am next? The shudders grow less pleasurable, but there's no escaping the power – and when Ted says, laughing as the dark-haired waitress comes up with a slice of dull quiche and a salad, that a woman he knows has taught him 'how to make the hairs on a person's neck stand up even if they are miles away!' I believe him without much difficulty. What to do, I think, as he suggests a trip to the zoo after lunch (this is at least unsurprising), what to do about the hairs on your own neck when you aren't miles away but right up close, against the granite cliff face, about to tumble down?

Instead of the zoo, we choose Holland Park and the peacocks. As I leave the restaurant I realise I'm on my own, and I go back to the Bar to see what has happened to my companion: has he disappeared again, as he did on arrival? There is no sign of him – then hey presto, he's out in the piazza in front of Julie's, the car door is already open. 'What a *lovely* man. I'm so pleased for you,' says the waitress, now behind the tall dark counter, a mermaid with yearning eyes, and I feel, for the first time, what it would be to find oneself wife, mistress or even occasional friend of this shaman. I get into the car before there is time to wonder what passed between my lunching companion and the girl. Back in the force-field of Ted's personality, it doesn't matter for long.

When feelings are heightened – and certainly every effort appeared to have been made to raise mine to fever pitch – it's hard to say afterwards what coincidences and correspondences were 'real' and what were imagined, encouraged by the conjuror busy preparing to saw the lady in half. The peacocks actually did strut with unaccustomed vigour and open their tails like fans at a ball, while the brown rabbits behind the fence in this most

tame and barricaded of parks ran for their lives (or
so it seemed to me) at the sight of the tall man, the
Rabbit Catcher, who would snap their little necks
and stuff them in the pocket of a pair of shabby
trousers before they could scuttle under a clump of
bamboo. People were as accommodating as the
birds and beasts. Smiles came from grumpy old
men in stained camel coats who hadn't in all
probability smiled since leaving Poland thirty-odd
years ago. Inquisitive, approving looks were shot at
him by young matrons, who remembered love,
perhaps, when they saw him walk by. Or – more
likely – romanticised but true, they dreamt of sex as
once they had enjoyed it with young husbands,
before the nine-to-five, the baby, the long
excruciating hours with push-chair in the park. Did
he seem so radiant, so sure of his ability to capture
hearts – quite alone and unconnected with the
nervous person at his side, the one who laughed
and looked up at him admiringly but all the while
fell deeper and deeper into a lake of fear? I felt this
must be the case: I was a prop, I could have been an
artificial woman, on display to demonstrate the
enduring appeal of the man who couldn't resist
women, despite the 'mayhem', as it was said, of his
past. But this was nonsense, of course. No-one in
Holland Park had any idea who the tall man was.
He simply radiated his own power and charm.

Fortess Road is a long, ugly road that climbs up

into North London by way of Tufnell Park. The flat
– despite my questions I never discover what or
why this flat actually is – is on the top floor of a
house that seems as long a toiling climb to the sky
as the traffic-roaring road is on its route through
suburbs to the North. Ted climbs behind me. He
overtakes when we have finally arrived at a
cramped top landing under the eaves, and with a
key that grates in the door he pushes his way in. I
follow. There is a small sitting-room, furnished only
with a Fifties-style basket chair – through an open
door I can see a large bed, rumpled sheets (the
obvious thought that a woman visits him here is
expelled from my mind), and piles of typescripts
and notebooks everywhere, floor, chair and bed. I
feel an interloper (it's true, then, as Olwyn had said,
that Ted comes to London to work: the farm in
Devon can be too demanding and distracting). This
is the lair (again the animal word) of an imagination
at full stretch – from here will come the story he
has promised for the magazine. I look down at my
summer-bare arms (it's hot today although still only
April) and see the white blemishes which have been
appearing there recently – grave-spots, as some
people like to call them, laughing at my concern. I
know the whiteness of death as I stare at this
pigment-absent visitation, and I think of the mono-
logue in the car on the way up to Tufnell Park – the
fourth-floor mansion flat in Baker Street pointed out

with 'I knew a pretty woman of forty who lived there.
She died' – and the talk of Thomas Hardy, which
had made me recall the line: 'Woman much missed,
how you call to me, call to me' and, reciting, stare
right at the driver's profile, to be answered, unexpectedly, with a great ogreish laugh. Why all the death?
And I remain with the image of the woman's dress
in that most haunting of Hardy's poems, 'her original
air-blue gown' singing in my head like an Aeolian
harp. I begin to surrender to a state that is both
sleepy and stunned – I'm hypnotised, I'm caged.

'The chair,' says Hughes, pointing to the
humble basketwork-with-back and arms of the
Fifties student, used either in the kitchen or as a
work table for anxious revision. 'Sylvia's last piece
of furniture . . . '

The Fiasco

There are some silences impossible to describe, so
noisy are they with thoughts, doubts, half-
remembered topics which may or may not prove
suitable in the event of social or sexual catastrophe,
and – frequently – loud, unspoken longings to
escape the scene.

How could it have been that I hadn't noticed
the sofa, up against the wall with the door leading to
the bedroom? – a sofa on which we now sit, Ted I
feel much nearer to me than anyone has ever been

before, perhaps because of his size, possibly due to the lurking fear that makes an adversary treble in stature in the eyes of his terrified foe? From far away I see myself, in this shabby little room in need of a coat of white paint, high above a city in which my whereabouts is entirely unknown. I sense the bed through the half-open door; we kiss; but I struggle for words, I must control my own response through speaking – somehow, my about-to-be lover senses this in return and stops me, saying, 'We're both too soaked in words, we've read everything, imagine we know nothing . . . ' and as he speaks I see in a jealous flash the 'bouncy' Australian girl with whom, so 'everyone' says, Hughes is conducting a full-time affair. How can I be like her? Yet, at the same time, this is hardly the moment to bemoan to myself the fact that I have most certainly not read everything. I'm largely uneducated – does he know? A mad impulse leads me to turn to him – teacher, mentor: the magic all writers need must surely come from him – and I feel the weight of the hundred times he's read each Shakespeare play – 'a hundred and one times, one time more than Peter Redgrove' he laughed as we ate lunch all those light years ago – and find I am, shamingly, no longer able to control my need to be seen not as a lover but as a promising pupil. 'Can you explain metaphor to me?' I say in a high, forced voice. Ted pulls back. I tell myself to stop, but it seems I must expose my

pathetic ignorance of the simplest term and lose
this moment of passion, as the women's magazines
would surely have it, at the same time.

When Ted has explained metaphor I find I am
already in the wide bed with grubby sheets. Our
bodies are pale – I think again of the bronzed
Australian, I am no contrast, pale as the man who
has so famously written of the Rape of Lucrece but
in my case without the learning or empathy with the
genius of Shakespeare. What am I, then? What is my
point? I know of Ted's admiration for Robert Graves
– but, apart from the pallor, I can hardly be seen as
The White Goddess. He has spoken of my friend
Caroline – Caroline Blackwood, who has the looks of
a drowned beauty and drinks, drinks, drinks . . . He
spoke as we drove up here of her stormy marriage
with Lowell – but affectionately, saying Lowell saw
in his new wife a creature risen from the sea. If Ted
compares – if he insinuates that he and I will be
such another couple, he a great poet, I a woman
whose talent needs encouragement and whose
family background is fraught with an inheritance
well-known to the land of the tabloids – then that is
who I am. But I don't know how to act it. And my
gift for saying the wrong thing at the wrong time has
indeed had its effect on the love-making: I swoon
with embarrassment as the scene collapses and the
room goes pointed and dark above Taurean
shoulders while outside the sun hides under a bank

of cloud and a wind and rainstorm begin to turn the sky a deep purple against fragile windowpanes.

The battle, I begin to realise, is not with me. I am the stand-in, the surrogate for the woman who did know everything and could write anything but lost the love she was unable to live without. She heard it galloping off like a horse – that line, in all Sylvia's poetry the most anguished, haunts me as loud as the hooves she heard that day; and I close my eyes, like a dead woman. No, I fight against the cheap melodrama of this bed.

'Sleep then,' Ted says.

But of course I don't. I know I have allied myself with the ghost, in Ted's mind at least: I have risen to eat him like air: he rues the day he took the woman born – though in a later year – seven days before his first wife to this eyrie, up the splintered stairs and past the sad rooms, all empty now (or so it seems, for I hear no movement anywhere in the exhausted building). He will not permit her/me to win – and he lies looking at me, Picasso's Minotaur mortally wounded, a ringlet of curled girls looking down and laughing at him from the stadium. Unbelievably, I make another literary allusion. Am I really so insecure that my loathsome autodidacticism must be brought forth in even the most unsuitable circumstances? 'Stendhal describes it in *De l'amour*,' I say. 'The Fiasco.'

*   *   *

I'm driven back to Notting Hill, past the mansion block in Baker Street where the 'pretty woman of forty' lived before she met her nemesis and died. Past the house where Thomas Hardy, as a young poet in London, fell in love with all the girls with chubby arms on the pavements of Westbourne Villas and Richmond. I think, as we drive, that Ted's pale American muse, Sylvia, followed by his dark lady – the beautiful Assia, who killed herself too – have combined to make a mythology from which he will, despite all his efforts, never be able to escape. Greek tragedy and the Cabbala form the mosaic of his supernatural beliefs. Any woman who becomes embroiled with him will find herself, like a Pompeiian victim, pressed in stone.

As we arrive in the Crescent with its trees just coming into leaf, a wild honking and cackling breaks out and a flock of geese flies overhead. We are just under their flightpath, as I remark, seeing Ted's eyes dream of their landing on the river. He asks me, as I climb from the car and stand a minute looking up at the house, if I've read of the habits of the greylag goose – a subject that's recently become much talked about, thanks to books by Konrad Lorenz. I say that I have. 'They are faithful to their first mate,' Ted says. 'I may be— ' and here he laughs at himself, then corrects his levity and falls serious, speaking so low I have to walk round the car to hear. 'I may, after all, be a greylag goose.'

* * *

Writing at night, as the spring turns to cold, rainy
summer. Daffodils in a glass on the work-table
replaced by anemones, bruised and half-dead, from
Portobello market. It's three weeks since I went to
Ted's flat, and the silence from him is louder than
the sound of a waterfall: it follows me everywhere,
begging me to make that one call no woman can, in
the end, resist making: the call that ends everything
or starts it up again.

Cowardly, I dodge the issue – it's less nerve-
racking than confronting the one person I both
dread and wish to confide in. (Besides, as people tell
me, Hughes has to change his phone number
frequently, to escape the vengeful American
feminists or prying journalists who would like to
pin him down.) I call my friend Dinny – she's from
another world, the world of SF, of sudden decisions
and instant reversals and she indulges my foibles,
even as she disapproves. She would be happy to
come round. Already I know, as I pull the I Ching
from its shelf, that confessions will be extracted
from me. But isn't that what I really want?

'So you're waiting till the tides are right,' Dinny
says laughing, as I throw coins on the floor and she
adds up their numbers. What can Confucius have to
say, I wonder distractedly, that will lead me out of
this new-found obsession for a man who cannot
even make a token communication after – after

what happened in North London? How much of a
fool have I become, to imagine these three-thousand-
year-old pronouncements can be interpreted to
soothe my self-imposed fever?

'It didn't work out,' I say.

In return I receive a long, amused stare. Now
comes the final shame for me, and I know it.
'Well . . .' comes the reply, which sounds as if the
water noise that pursues me had filled it to the
brim. 'You had *Splitting Apart* last time, if you
remember.' Dinny crosses and uncrosses her legs,
she is trim and looks far more conventional than
she really is. She lights one of her innumerable
cigarettes. Then, encouragingly: 'Now it's much
better . . .'

Why am I going in for all this?

Just as I write this in the Notebook where I set
down a jumble of ideas for the magazine, thoughts
on whatever comes into my head – and, most
importantly, ideas for stories and novels – a card
arrives from Ted. 'Missing you', it says in the spikey
black writing. He'll ring Monday and is coming to
London. I stare at the spiked handwriting and
realise I feel nothing at all.

What is it about women's confidences that
deadens, even temporarily extinguishes, the very
passion which has been confided? I conclude it's the
taboo of the 'other woman', whether she be sister,
mutual friend or total stranger. One woman

betrayed or abandoned, by opening herself out to a member of the same sex, creates a wall round a harem from which there is no escape. It occurs to me that some women prefer to complain about their treatment at the hands of brutal or insensitive lovers more than they enjoy the company of men. I hope, even at the oblique angle at which my relationship – if such it can be called – is proceeding with Ted, that this is not happening to me.

'If Sylvia's journals ever do see the light of day,' a poet I meet at a party says in a conversation in which the editing and publishing of Sylvia's work by her husband is disclosed, 'it won't be in this country. You know she made a bonfire of all Ted's papers?' And my informant rolls her eyes, in a sort of resigned horror.

Those words made me dream of fire all last night. Not the bonfire in Devon Sylvia made, of her unfaithful husband's poems and his edition of Shakespeare, but a fire in a tall grate in a house somewhere in London. Ted sits in a high-backed chair in front of the fire, which has a great fan of paper about to be lit, reaching almost up the chimney. I was cold with fear, even in the dream, for I knew, somehow, that these papers were in turn his wife's secret journals and most agonised cries of pain, expressed in the form of a poem, a diary, letters.

Soon after, I woke, knowing all was burnt.

For Ted, there can be nothing but the past, which he tries vainly to hide or to overlay with fresh experience.

Even though – as in my dream – he has committed to the flames the truth of what took place in his marriage to Sylvia, the truth is a salamander, always running from the fire into the open light of day.

All day I've been haunted by the burnt diaries – and Ted, in my dream turning in the high chair (wooden, five bars across the back) and looking at me as I have never seen him look: hostile, cold.

None of this prevents me from wondering when he will call.

The Real Blond

Lunch at Thompsons with the 'ebullient', 'larger than life' – what *is* the best way of describing Anthony Blond, or do those tags generally signal a publisher, anyway?

Blond is short, swarthy, infinitely enthusiastic about the prospect of making a book of *Bananas* stories, poems and articles. We all – that is, Julian, Rosalind, Tim and I – are like children in an orphanage as our new benefactor pours red wine, hums over the menu as if he sat in the Savoy, and

effortlessly transforms the unpretentious
Thompsons into a venue for business meetings.

Glasses are lifted: 'To the Youngest, the
Brightest, the Best,' toasts Blond, before going on to
explain that he and his partner Briggs habitually
chant this slogan when making a publishing
decision. It only reminds me that I'm older than
any of the *Bananas* team, by a long way; and as for
being the brightest and best, Julian informed me, as
we left the office and skirted the piles of old rubbish
bags which seem to have become a permanent
feature of Blenheim Crescent, that our typesetter
has just died of an overdose.

But hype springs eternal: we must eat up our
monkfish (pronounced by the French waiters like
'monocle') and promote, promote. I will make sure
John Sladek's 'After Flaubert' is included in the
anthology: it sends up contemporary wisdom, cliché
and banality with wicked accuracy. Also, Hilary
Bailey's cool-eyed tale of West London, 'Middle-class
Marriage Saved'.

Blond will find nuggets of world-weary
cynicism in his selection of the 'Youngest, the
Brightest and the Best'.

'I want you for no more than a year.' So declares the
man in the gloomy bar off Holland Park Avenue
(why did I bring him here? Dark-green Regency
stripes, polite, affected waiters: it just doesn't go
with Ted Hughes at all). 'We could . . . I could . . . '
hands which are broad and long, with fingers
that twitch as if remembering the tying of a
fisherman's knot, forming a noose, a pretty Mayday
concoction, move restlessly on the fake grain of
cocktail table wood . . . 'write' comes the word,
finally. Then a smile, from lips that are thin and
curved. 'Without a story there is no poem. Not even
a writer.'

I gaze across at the man who has just made
this odd proposition. Am I wanted for the giving
of hope? For comfort, when the words don't grow
or bloom? To provide the story, perhaps, to be
revealed in a poetic key so obscure no-one will
ever know we were together? Don't explain, a
voice says inside me. Poems don't explain. This is
where you start, from the place you can't
understand.

We finish our wine. It is cold and grey outside,
and some of the greyness has seeped into the bar.
Two middle-aged ladies sit discussing the sales.
Without a story, Ted says, there is no writer.
Without another writer, I believe he means, there

can never be a story. Our story will last no longer than a year. And my own returning smile becomes a burst of laughter – at the arrogance, the assumption of my consent, that lies behind this absurd request. I have young children, he a wife down in the house by the churchyard where Sylvia Plath wept at his leaving, lay awake on dark nights as love galloped off like a horse. What does he offer, he who knows the offers made by Fate and the price of acceptance?

Today, Ted looks even more like a primitive statue than ever. Maybe it's the genteel surroundings that emphasise the sense of being in the presence of a colossal being, a Mount Rushmore head weathered by the sun and rain. He rises and looks back at me, and catches my laughter, so the ladies in their mock pews stare up at him. 'I've booked a room in a hotel,' Ted says.

The Shout

Bayswater. A hotel that's as far from the architecture one would associate with the King of Verse as it's possible to get – no rough-hewn grandeur, no palace of ancient Greek Tragedy, just a grotty hotel with shifty short-term residents and that pervading acetone smell. And I wonder: why has Ted brought me here? And I look round the pebble-dash beige walls with something like panic. Is this where he brings those chosen for the half-hidden existence of the next in line as – and here I can't help smiling, despite my irrational fear – sub-mistress? Can he go on to talk of poetry in this room as he does everywhere else – in the park, the street, in his frosty eyrie in North London? Or does he change, metamorphose (I know him to be a lover of Ovid) into a ram, bull or swan, seizing his victim on the blank page of a hotel bed and transmuting her in turn into a tree or beast from which she will never be able to change back?

I think of the seediness and danger of the streets we have just walked down, with girls snatched by Arabs in waiting cars and gangs loitering by the doorways of banks and passport photo shops, and I feel myself in the most dangerous place of all. This, as the over-loud thumping of my heart tells me, must be the time to ask myself the question I have tried, with a pretence of humour or irony, a defensive denial of the real trouble I'm walking into, to prevent myself or anyone else from asking. What does Ted want from me? And, most important, what do I really want?

The question is answered before it can repeat its demands. There is no chance of speech, the time for explanations or wonderings is gone. I see the eyes, fixed on mine, and my last coherent thought is that I refuse to surrender, like a heroine in a Mills &

Boon romance. And then, knowing myself hypnotised, more helpless than the most docile and dumb of heroines, I succumb. The only trouble is – but it's much later that I am able to reflect at all on the sudden roughness, the abandonment of the tentative air of our last encounter – the trouble is, I'm not a heroine at all. I can't pretend to be a victim, either: what *do* I really want? Pure sensation, as the Lord Byron groupies must have desired, in order to find freedom in lives so constricted no woman – no Western woman – would stand for it today? If so, why should I need it, with my 'free' life style? Is all this merely a matter of self-indulgence, a way of passing time as gamblers do, by visiting the casino and risking losing all?

Steps in the passage outside the door. Shuffling, a scraping of key in lock, then, as the key obviously doesn't fit, a knocking, loud and insistent, on the flimsy wood which separates us from the rest of the world.

I lie transfixed: I see secret police, ambulance men, all the servants of accident and danger. 'They' have come for us – it's the way being with Ted has one thinking, for in his universe there is nothing humdrum or ordinary, like a mistaken room number or a wrongly collected key. I am becoming like that, I decide, I fear the worst, and, as Ted so often underlines, if you fear the worst it is bound to befall you. What I had no knowledge of, before, was the thunder this man can produce, when he is disturbed or angry: the tiny, anonymous room rattles with the sound of his shout.

'*What do you want?*' This, so loud a great silence seems to descend on the hotel with its little canopy of grubby glass, and as far as the street, where even the traffic appears to go quiet at the Jove-like resonance of his voice.

More shuffling, then (not surprisingly) a scampering. The intruders have fled. Taxis growl by the kerb outside; the stink of kebab rises to our first-floor window and pokes in through a broken ventilator duct. The hypnotic calm is broken We are back where we were before; though how long ago this was I have no idea. We're returned from our mythic shapes to two people – what do *we* possibly want?

'You know, they're making a film of Robert Graves's story "The Shout"?' Ted says. He's lying on his back, a fallen mountain. The room, with its pink nylon frilly lampshade on the mock-mahogany bedside table, and the fitted cupboard from which a wire protrudes onto a violently purple, tufted carpet, is fast beginning to look far too confining for him. I rise, reminding myself I have my own decisions to make. I hardly hear the rest of what he is saying and I turn, exasperated by the self-confident air he seems to possess, just when the problems of my own life revisit me – along with guilt, of course. There's always plenty of that.

'I am "The Shout",' Ted says, and he laughs – so I find myself laughing too. Little wonder they cast this man as the maker of the Shout – the sound, like the voice of Pan when men still believed in the spell of fear the god could cast, which can turn bones to stone and freeze the blood. No-one but Ted could persuade a modern audience that a voice can wreak such havoc in the world.

'Why don't we go to Scotland?' he now says, casual, still unmoved by the growing claustrophobia of the room. Afternoon has passed to evening, the passage outside responds with a glare of strip lighting which comes under the ill-fitting door. 'To the Hebrides,' Ted goes on. 'Shall we go there?'

I walk to the door, push down the handle, both cold and sweaty to the touch. I say I must get home. Ted follows me a few minutes later (I wait in the passage, by a row of doors, for him: have all the occupants of these identical rooms heard The Shout? Do they cower in fear, lest a murderer has come amongst them?) We walk out, he transformed into an unexceptional man, a commercial traveller, for the purpose of walking past the little office with its plastic roses and frosted-glass cubicle door, I – as always – too tall and too noticeable to escape a hostile glance from the receptionist in there.

'Scotland,' says Ted. He likes the word, he forces me back to my Scottish past as we stand on

the pavement, lit by pink fluorescent lights, the
patisseries humming with the early-evening sound
of veiled women shopping for their families.

We part on the corner of Queensway. I have
learnt not to follow his departures with my eyes, in
case he looks back and construes my searching gaze
as a bad omen for the future.

But do I want a future? Is this meant to be the
beginning of the 'story'? And is it programmed to
last for 'no longer than a year'?

Bountiful Bragg

I've been lying low, trying to write *The Bad Sister*, a
novel which takes as its inspiration James Hogg's
Confessions of a Justified Sinner. It's a book of
doubles, of female doubles, and has as its centre the
belief held by ultra-feminists that they are above
moral judgement. It was Heathcote who told me
that somewhere in Notting Hill there is a large,
dilapidated house full of ferocious women with
their love-children, all of whom are given the
surname Wild. From this comes the name of my
anti-heroine: Jane Wild.

Money for the magazine has dropped to an all-
time low. Despite having persuaded the distribution
manager of W. H. Smith to take us on, despite the
Arts Council grant which was awarded with issue
No. 3, of £3,000 a year, we can barely pay

contributors or printers. Rosalind toils on at the office, as do various other part-time helpers, but the amount of incoming mail is gigantic. We are getting pretty well known, and a recent praising comment in *Time Out* from Melvyn Bragg inspired me to send a message to him that we are forced to close down for financial reasons. Bragg, chairman of the Arts Council, handsome and roughly suave, if such a combination is possible, comes over from the South Bank not too well pleased with my ploy. He says he'll hold various meetings and we are in fact allotted a slightly larger stipend – but I shouldn't think he'll look me in the eye if we meet again.

Going On Too Long

We have finally arrived! – a *Bananas* evening at the
National Theatre set in motion by Michael Kustow
and taking place at the Cottesloe at 6 p.m. Will
anyone come? But, on crossing the river and going
into the grim, zoo-like building, all seems brightness
and excitement. Flyers announce our writers
reading from their work, and people are actually
buying tickets for the event. I remember Jimmy
saying that some of the writers in *Bananas* had been
'rolling their pennies down Ladbroke Grove' without
making much of a splash, until they were placed in
the magazine. I wonder, modestly, if he refers to
himself, at all – it's certainly true that Ballard has
graduated, if that's the word, from brilliant SF writer
to acclaimed mainstream author, while writing his
extraordinary stories for the magazine. But he
probably doesn't think that way – and now the
lights dim and we all rush in to the auditorium.

I suppose the worst flop of the evening must
have been Heathcote's attempt at a Maskelyne &
Devant-like act, levitating his daughter China on
stage. It failed utterly. Jenny Joseph, an excellent
poet (though when I introduced her once thus she
reprimanded me sharply, saying 'a poet' had no
need of a qualifying adjective) was not easy to hear.

Ballard triumphed with his reading: he no longer sounds like a specialist announcing worse-than-expected results of a colonoscopy when he reads aloud. Everyone loved it. But Heathcote climbed on the stage again and wouldn't get off, despite the National Theatre's next scheduled performance – and I couldn't get him to leave. I was tapped repeatedly on the shoulder from behind by Michael Kustow. Finally we all went our several ways home – but now there's someone else who is likely never to want to have dealings with me again.

Caroline Blackwood at Home

'Are you Mum's best friend? I think she's tried to kill herself.'

It's late at night; I'm about to go to bed, and the phone call and odd question from Evgenia, Caroline's eldest daughter, set my mind spinning, before I say I'll come round at once, another 'best friend' with me. I call a cab, and search frantically for cash in my bag, 'She's tried to kill herself' singing in my ears like something on a radio you can't turn off.

Caroline Blackwood had been a close friend – perhaps they had been in love – of my elder brother, Colin. My first 'grown-up' outing had consisted of lunch in a private room at Brown's Hotel with, as well as my brother, a young man

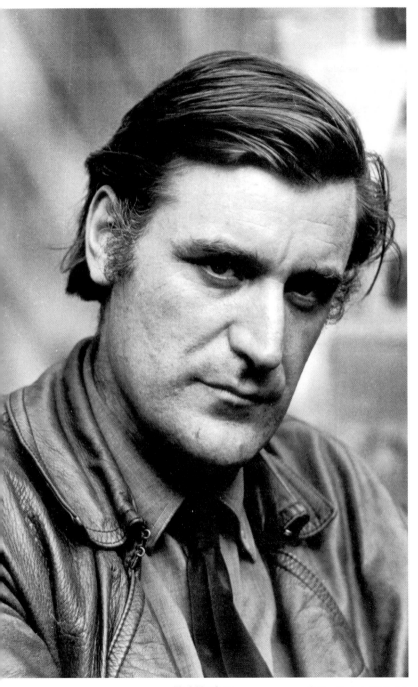

Ted Hughes   © Fay Godwin / Network

Above: Rosalind Delma
at work and talk.
*Courtesy of Rosalin
Delma*

Left: Emma Tennant in
Notting Hill.
© *Dmitri Kasterin*

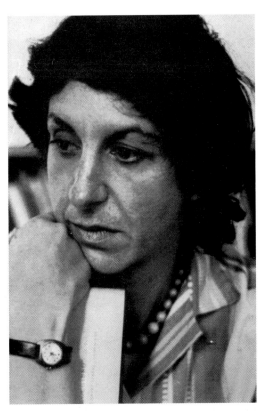

Right: Elaine Feinstein.

Below: Angela Carter.

Above: Caroline Blackwood.

Left: Bruce Chatwin.
© *Jane Brown/Arena*

Picador 10th Birthday celebrations, left to right: Tim Binding, Michael Herr, Salman Rushdie, Bruce Chatwin, Clive James, Adam Mars-Jones, Mike Petty, Russell Hoban, Hugo Williams, Tim Maschler, Oliver Sachs; seated: Sonny Mehta, Emma Tennant.

Harold Pinter and Tim Owens in a Dorset Garden.

Left: Claud Cockburn in Chelsea before the move.

Below: Julian Rothenstein with books from his imprint Redstone Press.

Courtesy of Julian Rothenstein

, Blenheim Crescent, Notting Hill, just before *Bananas* took up residency.

Above: JG Ballard.
© *Fay Godwin / Network*

Left: Heathcote
Williams in the Open
Head Press office
above *Bananas.*
© *Ron Reid 1979. Courtesy*
of Richard Adams

called Johnny Norton, and two beauties, one dark
and the other Caroline, who was fair with a
mermaid's huge green eyes. Both beauties took me
into the Ladies before lunch and spat into little
boxes of mascara, as I, fourteen years old, watched
gravely. Caroline's eyes got bigger and bigger, as she
outlined them with the spitty brush. She must have
been eighteen or nineteen, not so much older than
me, but a century of bohemian sophistication
divided us. I noticed her hair was dirty and her skin
a chalky white. A short time later, Lucian Freud
painted her when they were married. My brother
bought the picture. Caroline's skin and the sheets of
the bed where she lies, in the painting, are deathly
white.

The reason I can't really answer to the
description 'best friend' – or answer Evgenia
properly on the subject – is because I saw so little of
her mother in all the years she lived in America,
after leaving her first, childless, marriage to Lucian
Freud and marrying the composer Israel Citkovitz,
bearing him three daughters. I have only a faint
idea, through stories told by friends, of Caroline's
life in New York. I know her writing, which is
brilliant, black, like a squid's ink squirted on the
issues of the day, or, as in her best fiction, on
relatives and friends who are thinly disguised
recipients of her lacerating wit. I know her well,
really, only since she came to London and installed

herself and her family (she has left the girls' father by now) in a high-up duplex in Redcliffe Square. She met and went off with the poet Robert Lowell, when he was teaching at Essex, and she married him in America. But it's true – still pondering Evgenia's question – that we have become close since she settled in Earl's Court; if 'settled' can ever describe the movements of this unwilling member of the Guinness clan.

I know the relationship with Lowell (who died just under two months ago) had been terrifying to Caroline, his manic attacks impossible to endure – like a massive weight dropped on a highly strung instrument: one could almost hear the straining of the wires as she tried to cope. And she drinks – vodka which soon oozes from the corners of those great kohl-rimmed eyes and makes her talk, often funny and incoherent, boil down to a kind of grim pastiche of Society gossip, much of it involving her hated mother, the dragon Marchioness, Maureen Dufferin. Most things, from domestic crises – 'I *know* why Sylvia [Plath] killed herself: the nanny didn't turn up' – to real or imagined brush-offs from in-laws – 'You know that song "*Ever* seen a lady/Go this way and that way?/*Ever* seen a lady go this way and that?" Well it describes her perfectly' – trigger Caroline's scorn. Yet she is kind-hearted and loving to her friends. I'm glad to be her best friend, if that's how she sees me.

I go with Francis Wyndham to the Gothic pile
that is the house in Redcliffe Square. The poor
daughter lets us in, leads us to an upper storey, the
door to its staircase bolted against rescuers. We
pound and bang, calling out her name.

There's only one thing for it: call the police. I
see visions of Caroline, as white as she is in the
Freud painting, but lying flat, insensible on the
pillows instead of propped on one arm. The eyes
are closed. It's unbearable, and I misdial in my
panic, waking an innocent sleeper miles away.
Then a faint noise comes from behind the locked
door. '*Caroline*!' Francis shouts. A shuffling sound;
as in an early rendering of the madwoman-in-the-
attic scene in *Jane Eyre*, the door opens and a bleary
face looks round, bird's-nest hair and a grubby
nightie completing the picture. 'I'm *terribly*
sorry . . .'

We drink coffee, the relieved daughter going
down to a piled-high kitchen to rescue filter jug and
cups. We watch Caroline having a vodka. Finally, we
make our way out into the night. I can't help
reflecting that, even in these most undignified of
circumstances, it is impossible to forget Caroline's
talent and unflinchingly accurate eye. Whether
writing about bodies in bin-liners, during a recent
gravediggers' strike in Manchester, or underlining
the layers of greed and hypocrisy that support her
upper-class background (Anglo-Irish, Old

Ascendancy, Guinness millions to bring the necessary touch of evil), Caroline never does anything other than tell the frequently grisly truth.

We go back in silence to Notting Hill. For all of what's left of the night I lie half awake, half asleep, seeing in bursts the sudden death of Robert Lowell in the taxi in New York that carried him back to his first wife, Elizabeth Hardwick. I see his slumped figure, the door of the cab opening, the parcel he has brought from London with him falling out into the road. 'You know what was in the parcel?' Caroline says. We're sitting together in my house, a week or so after her husband's fatal heart attack. Her enormous eyes swim with the cruelty and irony of life, and she laughs. 'The painting of me – you know.'

I see at once the picture she means. It's the one of her in bed, of course, the painting by Lucian Freud. 'He was taking it to be valued,' Caroline says. 'Isn't it the *worst*?'

Monsieur Hulot

I want to try and set down some of my thoughts about Ted Hughes and poetry; but tonight is as interrupted as the day: all I can do is write what happened earlier. How, whether you think you know someone or not, there are surprises, in this case a sense of a different identity from the one I'd supposed; and a shaft of that valuable and unexpected quality in so serious and doom-laden a poet, humour.

It's so easy to see the poems, limestone carvings, ancient oak forests, etc. of England, in Ted – his own lines coming, as he says, from silence, from a world where there is nothing and he must wrestle to extract them anew each time – that it is a jolt to recognise, suddenly, that there is more of the Greek in him than the Norseman or Celt. *Gaudete*, with its Satanic vicars, its Stanley Spencer fairyland of good and evil, obscures the myths and Homeric epics which seem to belong more to him than this strained (and much disliked by critics) latest narrative poem. Ted is the magician who transforms; the master of metamorphosis. I saw it in him today, as we sat in an (understandably empty) little restaurant at the far end of Clarendon Road, the roar of Holland Park Avenue deadened by bunched gingham curtains and scuffed velvet chairs. Unappealing dishes were set before us, but the total lack of an audience, of the quick, surreptitious glance (Ted is either recognised instantly, or so remarkable in appearance that no-one can resist a stare), clearly made the choice of place to meet worthwhile.

Yet there's something restless in him today;

and, as I come to realise, something in me that won't accommodate to this. I've already been asked, 'Have you seen the film – the theatre troupe that goes all over Greece – the film by Theo Angelopoulos?' and I've replied that yes, I have seen *The Travelling Players*. By now the wandering nature of Ted's thoughts and mine, unspoken, has taken us across the Ionian Sea and into the Peloponnesus, through musty ports and over moorland that must remind us both and separately of our home ground. Beyond that I see him, as he comes into focus in the treeless landscape and stands looking down over cliffs at a steely sea, as the man who has travelled so far and fast he has lost himself: there have been deaths, some inscribed as murders, on the perfect blue slate of the sky, and, however far down the valley he must go, he wants to find his way home.

'That film,' says Ted, emphasising the words with a great slap on the table (even this bringing no response from the silent kitchens at the dark rear of the room), 'has opened a door for me.' And I remember, pulled back into the present from my own dream of a young woman, King Alcinous's daughter, writing in her room in the palace, of the exploits of Odysseus, that Ted has himself travelled in the Middle East, inventing a new language for a theatre; that there is nothing he doesn't know of the roots of tragedy, before he has had to live out his own; and that he must belong, whether he accepts it or not, more in the shadow of the *Oresteia* than in Olde England. I feel my powerlessness in the face of both knowledge and experience, and my head bends down, stopping just above a bright tablecloth, where bread, nervously pulled apart, lies like a bombed village on the red and yellow squares. Aren't I to travel, too? – I sense the world of war, and mountain distances. If I'm to stay quietly in a room, I protest in silence, I prefer to do so without the dominating presence of Ted.

This is as useless as my own apprehensions about myself, I know: no-one asked me to stay quietly in a room, or to suffer the superiority of one with whom there are no ties. All the same, I rebel. When the meal is finally eaten and we stumble from artificial darkness into light, to the rush of Holland Park Avenue traffic and the tall houses and trees, I step into the car as unwilling as a prisoner. (I'm self-conscious too, of course: after all, I'm hardly forced at gunpoint to drive in the dead streets and cul-de-sacs of this rich area. I need only raise my hand and the car will stop. I'll be alone on the wide, well-swept pavement).

'Shall we go and lie down?' says Ted, who has noticed nothing of my mood – or, if he has, doesn't show it.

The words are unfortunate, building further a picture of passivity in which, like an Arab woman, I am closeted behind walls, living and waiting only for the occasional visit of a man. The talk of Greece, it seems, has made me want to run as far as I can from this 'arrangement', if that is what it is. I certainly do want to get out of the car – and I also know I don't want to go home.

'There's a room,' Ted says; and, for the first time, I wonder at the refusal, by one whose veins of sensibility are almost visible beneath the surface of his skin, to feel or try to understand my mood of rebellion and anger. But then, why should he? I am seen as adventurous, free – this is what I must want, as much as he does. The sound of the voice of reason – even though it's my own – maddens me all the more, however. Possibly, Ted's own description of the total wordlessness of the world he confronts when he writes has shown me the far greater silence imposed on women – even now, even here – than any struggle with expression Ted could ever know. 'I can't,' I say, as the car turns again, down one of the endless one-way hills and banks. 'I'll get out here. Please.'

Ted leans across the passenger seat and gazes up at me as I stand by a flowery hedge, still scowling. He thinks it's physical, no doubt . . . and as I sense the limitations exercised by a woman's body, the need to escape, to march on the hills of an unexplored country, grows stronger still. It's unfair, the child that has surfaced in me screams. Ted may

walk Greece, sail the seas, fight his way off islands
where the women wait to lure him into their arms. I
– in some mythical way that I know to be true –
cannot. At least, for all he professes to believe of
me, not in his eyes.

Inevitably, I'm disarmed. The enemy who
stares up at me from the car window smiles –
almost in sympathy. A comic character begins to
emerge: in the stooped shoulders and half-stern,
half-laughing face now shown in profile to me, a
transformation is taking place. Gears clash
clumsily, as the car pulls away. 'I'll feel like
Monsieur Hulot, going to cancel at the hotel,' he
calls back as he turns and the car rises steeply out
of sight.

We advertised in *The Times* for a backer – and,
amazingly, we got one. At least, a half-backer – a Mr
J. Bates will put up £5,000 to enable *Bananas* to
continue, but there's no promise of a stable future.
(Nor are there strings attached: we are most
grateful.)

Mr Bates came round and we all, for some
reason, talked about our schooldays. Perhaps
because our new angel has the appearance of being
hardly out of school himself. We ended the evening
knowing little more about each other than at the
start – but already, like a dying plant, the magazine
perks up at the injection of cash.

And Mr Bates will continue to read excellent fiction and poetry: there are glowing reactions to Angela Carter's story in the last issue, and Sara Maitland is writing with great clarity and vigour. Tim Owens, with 'The Night it Rained', shows an undoubted talent for the mysterious and enigmatic. And Thomas M. Disch, along with John Sladek, is a totally different voice. Both come from the great flat plains of Minnesota (but urban, computer-led, affectless).

In the future, Bruce Chatwin's 'Until my Blood is Pure' will transport Mr Bates – and many readers, one hopes – from the middle classes-in-Hampstead we're told is the staple English novel to an African tale of syphilis in Douala.

But will there ever be enough readers to augment the Bates investment? Five thousand was the optimum level stated by Cyril Connolly when discussing the prospects of a serious literary magazine, such as *Horizon*. We have little more than three thousand readers – so I calculate, at least. Is there no change in the past thirty years, then?

But these moans are the usual lullaby of those trying to run a magazine. We are grateful to Mr Bates.

The Practise of Magic

After another long silence, cards start to arrive from Ted – he is 'tramping the hills' of England, in his

visits to schools, to children who must learn to love
and understand poetry, or he's 'had three weeks
knocked out' in an attack of 'flu on a visit to Paris.
He sends encouragement for the book I'm writing,
my book of doubles, shadows and good and evil
women, much inspired by his own obsession with
the occult, though in my case the interest lies in the
thin boundary between deep psychoanalysis and
magic. Without him, as I'm aware, the novel would
never have got off the ground.

We next meet in a restaurant near where I live
whose name is irresistible to Ted, La Pomme
d'Amour, and he hands me a book, a modest
hardcover in a black jacket, *An Introduction to
Hermetics* – in smaller letters below are the words
'The Practise of Magic'. On the title page he writes
his inscription, adorning my name with the wings
of a bird, to denote freedom, and the 'd'' of Ted with
a dragging anchor, to underline his trapped state,
tied at home. As we drink our wine, an
acquaintance from the past approaches our table
and he introduces me as 'Emma, who runs a paper I
write for. She lives up and down the world, while I
still live in Devon,' and I open the book of magic
he's given me and wonder if one of the spells within
couldn't carry him away from the house where he
lived so long with Sylvia Plath and continues to live
now, surrounded by memories of her.

What doesn't occur to me – not fully, at least –

is how I'm being indoctrinated into what Ted's detractors love to refer to laughingly as the 'black arts'. I am being taught to read horoscopes (my own, so near to Plath's day and month of birth, has caused particular excitement). I must understand portents, ward off the evil eye, study the electro-magnetic forces within the cranium, so I can control the actions of others. Also, more important, I can by these means bring up words when I write. They must be drummed from the depths by magic. I will be liberated, at last, from the constrictions of my upbringing and education. My 'story', my confession, will finally, like invisible ink warmed by fire, show on the page before me.

'Where on earth do you get a book like this?' I say, when the acquaintance has wandered away – not without casting an over-interested gaze in my direction. For all his other-worldly persona, adopted when the subject of occult phenomena comes up, I see that Ted is uneasy at having been seen here. As if he could hide – but too late – he lifts a vast tome that is the wine list, and buries his head in it. 'Near the British Museum – Watkins – he has all these kind of arcane volumes.' Ted's voice is muffled by the thick parchment with its long list of Pouilly Fuissés, Château Margaux, and champagnes so expensive they could keep a family for weeks – nevertheless, as if in bravado after this unwelcome recognition from his 'real' life, he goes ahead and

orders a bottle of Dom Perignon. It would be
churlish of me to say I don't much like champagne,
so I stay silent, trying to look as if I appreciate his
generosity. '*The Chymical Wedding*,' Ted is saying as
I look up and meet the eye of the man who has
greeted him, standing by the door before leaving La
Pomme d'Amour – his look suggests a prurient
curiosity further inflamed by the prompt arrival of
ice bucket, gold-topped champagne bottle and
obsequious waiter. 'A book in fourteenth-century
High Dutch,' says Ted. 'You should read it.' And
there and then he dives under the table and pulls
from a battered bag a book in manuscript form. The
incomprehensible early language jumps out from
the page as he hands it over to me. By the time all
this has taken place the unwelcome guest at our
own chemical romance has vanished, the soft swish
of the restaurant door sounding as he goes out into
the street. Ted relaxes. In his view, at least, he has
been seen handing a manuscript to an editor –
though how or why this explains the champagne it
would be hard to say, High Dutch of the Middle
Ages being in all probability not destined for the
bestseller lists.

It's impossible not to speculate, when this
display of extravagance takes place, on the
accusations levelled at Hughes and the Plath Estate
– especially of course by American feminists – that
money earned by the poet who killed herself after

Hughes's treatment of her is squandered for his own personal pleasure. Certainly, Ted loves food – no sooner has the Dom Perignon been opened than a whole sea bass arrives, cooked on a bed of twigs and fennel leaves that resembles the mythical kingfisher's nest afloat on the sea in halcyon days. One is inclined to reflect, when presented with all these luxuries, that Ted loves comfort and a fine table – but that he also loves to share his spoils. I glance down at the *Introduction to Hermetics*, and, for all the soft lights, the champagne and the fine food, I feel the by-now-familiar thrill of fear. Yet I know myself well enough to realise I won't care about this in one minute's time; for Ted has only to tell me a story and I am as enraptured – and frightened in the true, good sense – as a child.

Today he talks not of memory – of the mnemonics of the ancient orators which he loves to recount: the pillars in a colonnade on which in imagination they placed their words, the theatre of ancient Greece – but of something more ancient still, so primitive it goes right under the skin, so I sit silent as he tells the tale.

'It's a Bushman's story,' Ted says simply. A young man in Africa is crossing a great wide expanse when he is seen and followed by a lion. He runs as fast as his legs will carry him, and climbs up the first tree he comes to, hiding along the trunk 'like this' – Ted makes the shape of the young man, and then the fork of a tree. 'But the lion sees him there. And, although it cannot pull him down, it sees his arm dangling and licks it, licks the young man. Later, when the lion has gone, the young man returns to his village. He cannot go to his own hut – all the villagers know the lion has been after him, and they hide him, always changing the hut where he lies low. But,' says Ted, as he sees me cringe back with the inevitability of the end of the story, 'but the lion comes to the village and goes from hut to hut, looking for the young man. It doesn't want anyone else, it wants *him.*'

'And?' I say, looking at the waiter who stoops over us now with espresso coffee, as if he is about to be eaten, as if he should run to save his own life.

'The lion found the young man and killed him,' Ted finishes off. He laughs.

Does Ted enjoy presenting himself as an ogre, a black magician who finds his victim, licks her into submission with his wiles and looks and charm, and then follows her ruthlessly to the kill? It's impossible to say. But certainly, he appears to accept the reading of his own horoscope – the 'good and evil fame' to which he believes he is destined for the rest of his days.

I saw, perhaps, an example of the latter after we had left the moneyed comfort of the Pomme d'Amour and gone out into a rainy, chilly summer's afternoon. A poet – I recognised him as Tom, a schizophrenic who had visited me in the magazine office, bringing with him a black attaché case containing only, and terrifyingly, a long-bladed kitchen knife – stopped us not a hundred yards from the gates to Holland Park. It was Ted he wanted. Mesmerised by Ted and food and wine, shuddering at the Bushman's tale I had just heard, I stood back on the wide pavement as Tom hung on Ted's arm, gesticulating and muttering, trying to drag him into the traffic, generally causing a disturbance which passers-by stared at in alarm.

'Let's go.' Ted's voice was angry, softer than I'd heard it, but more menacing. He indicated to me to open the car door – we had both been pulled along to where Ted's car was parked, and with his free hand he had deftly unlocked the door. 'Get in,' Ted said to me. 'In the back.' It was a two-door car and I didn't want to obey, for the madman (as Tom clearly was: like a stage lunatic, he was foaming at the mouth) was being ushered into the front passenger seat, and the prospect of being penned in with him was far from enticing. 'Open my bag,' Ted hissed at me, throwing the rubbed old satchel onto the back seat beside me 'He's followed me up from Devon. He plagues me there. First he slept in my barn for a year, then in the field, now when I go up to town he somehow gets here too.'

'What do I do?' I said, by now genuinely terrified. Tom was locked into the front of the car,

his seatbelt fastened against his will, and he twisted
and turned in an effort to free himself.

'Open the bag and take out a sheet of paper'
Ted spoke so fast I could barely understand him. But
– somehow – I undid the satchel and pulled a
pristine sheet of A4 from its depths

'Here.' Ted took Tom by the shoulder and held
him in a clamp. A pen-knife appeared in his right
hand. '*Look*!' Ted said in a voice that would have
raised the dead. Even though he was in a small car
with the windows closed, a woman with a push-
chair veered wildly to the edge of the pavement
when the voice sounded from behind glass. '*Look* at
this' – to Tom.

A silence fell. I sensed the power in the
gesture then performed, the terrible, symbolic
strength.

Ted's pen-knife cut through the white sheet of
paper diagonally, a clean cut which separated the
unwritten page into two identical halves. Tom sat
looking at it as if a living creature had been
sacrificed before his eyes – or his soul had been cut
in two.

'He won't trouble us again,' Ted said, when he
had released the poet, who shambled off aimlessly
into the Holland Park Avenue crowd.

Nights are drawing in again but, for the first time I
can remember, I feel none of the excitement that

comes with the ending of a year. The leaves are staying longer than usual this year on the few trees that have escaped disease and surgical treatment, in this area of communal gardens, small woods and streets where householders, aping country-dwellers, stride to bonfire sites and compost heaps.

The leaves are bright, fragile, and some are as thin as glass. I stare mournfully out at them, yearning for a return to the ordinary – for even the mild autumnal scene seems by now pregnant with meaning, coincidence, intent. I am caught in the spell cast by Ted, the master magician, and there is no way out.

But I flinch from looking in the volume of hermeneutics. The School of Witches he would have me join leads, I know, to madness, despair, suicide. The devil is everywhere. Ted plays with him, and knows his discipline. I can't do it, even – the devil's promise – if the words I wrote were suddenly lit by genius.

I see my novel, *The Bad Sister*, as a terrifying portent of the schizophrenic world into which I am drawn. 'Bathed in black magic' is Angela Carter's epithet when I send it to her, and this will appear on the cover. It sounds as cosy as the box of chocs and crackling autumn fire it conjures up. In fact, my examination of the female double is already surrounded by inexplicable coincidences and an aura which is 'magical', but not in the fashion-word sense.

A side of me I had forgotten, or certainly neglected, begins to surface and then is pushed under by the sheer force of Ted's persona. This side of me loves the light of the rational and laughs at the superstitions of the medieval world. *Bananas* sends up – inimitably in the fiction of John Sladek – the fashionable horrors of the world we live in: astrology, 'miracle cures', radiation theories, crazy conspiracy books. What is happening to me? I must return to where I belong, for all the lure of the Gothic dream.

Theatre of Cruelty

A very different occasion at the National Theatre
from Heathcote's levitation and my own
unsuccessful attempt at getting the idea of an avant-
garde magazine in this country off the ground
(despite my explanations of why we have come too
late in the day to merit a manifesto, people are
suspicious of an enterprise like *Bananas* without a
clear declaration of aims, Surrealist, Dada, etc.).

So it was a relief to slip into a world of poets
and writers who don't need anything at all 'unusual'
spelt out; and last night, the evening for Modern
Poetry in Translation at the Lyttelton, went a long
way towards exploring that 'path straight to the
centre' – or, another expression of Ted's, 'opening an
impossible door' which connects the mundane and
the spiritual, understands the horrors of the
Holocaust and can at the same time laud a flower in
bloom.

János Pilinszky was there; and the Israeli poet
Amichai, with his poem, sad and funny and
profound, of 'losing the weight of a son'. Ted had
been responsible for many of the translations, and
was in charge of the evening. I just wish, as I think
of it, and of the way I shall think of it in future – of
the gratitude of the poets, the sheer joy of Amichai

at finding himself in London, his mutters of delight
at the landmarks on the way there and back: Regent
Street, Eros in Piccadilly, the great dark swathe of
Hyde Park – I can only wish, as I'm sure I shall
wish for a very long time, that the evening had not
then gone on in the way it did.

I suppose things must have reached a point
with Ted where a part of me was no longer capable
of dissembling, of holding back.

We left the theatre, and walked out into a night
without rain. The Feinsteins, pluckier than most,
had brought their car and I went with them. The
underground car park miles from the auditorium
where we had sat enthralled by the words of the
Hungarian and Israeli poets, seemed to my
overwrought imagination a kind of Hell, cold and
shadowy – and, as I knew with a sinking heart, Hell
because I wasn't with the one person I wanted to be
with, I was alone in the Underworld, without Ted.
Was he missing me, too? But this, as I knew, was
childish in the extreme. Weren't we all to meet for
dinner?

'Lobster!' Amichai had cried out when a fish
restaurant in the West End was given as the
destination. And they all laughed – Elaine and
Arnold, and others who knew shellfish is banned in
Israel and it must be years since Amichai had tasted
it. 'Yes,' Ted said with his laugh, enjoying the
prospect of the dinner, loving the poet who can

express the subtle and saddest of feelings, for celebrating the imminent arrival before him of a plate of lobster. And – looking at me from the corner of his eye, restraining his smile, lowering his voice (but not quite enough to prevent his wife from hearing) – 'See you there.'

So why am I afraid and unhappy now, in this Hades below water – or so it seems, from the dripping roof, the rust, the cars that look as if they have ferried their owners to their last port of call? What do I dread, in this channel of the dead where history's crude actors walk between the river's banks, jostled by the poor, the unknown dead, the plasterer, the builder who fell today from the roof? That I will join them? That, if I don't obey this most compelling of men, I shall die?

I should have then decided to extricate myself, and go home. I hear Ted's words, when he speaks of his own home existence, casual and dismissive: 'I? Oh, I'm in hospital' – I know that, in alluding in this way to his wife, a nurse, he betrays his domestic happiness, he deceives *her*. But what am I doing, conniving at this? And – worse, the banality of it all makes me stumble against the battered mudguard of the finally discovered Feinstein car – don't all married men talk to the 'other woman' in this way? Don't most men, anyway, prefer a marriage that has them, chief patient, centre of attention, in hospital, to the competition and strain of life with an equal, a woman with a talent, a lustrous ego? 'It was all such mayhem' – Ted's sister's words come back to me, as I step disconsolately from puddle to tinny car and the engine does the wheezing and spluttering this dank basement exacts from it. Why on earth would more mayhem be on the cards? Yet Ted, without doubt, is inviting little else.

I'll look back on the evening and see the car, and the painful effort to park near Manzi's in Piccadilly, and the side-street where, bathed in shadows once again, we start our quick, excited walk. We'll join the King, I thinking of a summer evening, a party on a Hampstead lawn, where Ted and I are standing together (we've only recently met for the first time) and an American poet, a woman, points at us and says to her husband, loud enough for us to hear: 'The King and Queen!' And I decide – I have already decided, I think guiltily – that I shall tonight most certainly take the King.

The table on Manzi's first floor is long and L-shaped. I'm embarrassed to see that the 'head table' has one chair left empty, and that it's opposite Ted: his wife is placed next to him. The Feinsteins go with cries of friendship to join people further down – why, as I ask myself today, why did I not insist on going with them, I who travelled so slowly in their company from the watery car park, a river's breadth away? Why – as it emerged I was set on doing – must I nudge and (practically) wink: why does a strange hilarity overcome me? Why, as I press my knee against Ted's, do I care not at all who sees or becomes aware of my improper actions, when all I seem to want – and do in fact almost at once receive – is an answering burst of mirth? There cannot be any reason for the folly – and cruelty – of what I do, other than a desire for a brazen announcement to be made. But an announcement of what, exactly?

I wish I could record the joy of the Israeli poet eating his first lobster for years, or admit to consuming more than a mouthful of the fish I must have ordered – sole or plaice? – already it vanishes from mind. But I cannot. I have a wager with myself. He will come back to my house tonight, when the meal is finished. What on earth do I imagine will happen to his wife?

So it comes about. As in a dream – alas, still the dream of tarot King and Queen, of good fortune and bright skies – we drive to Notting Hill. I feel my luck holding out, I shrug when Arnold, bowed over the wheel, proclaims that 'Ted won't have come here'; I smile, gracious and distant, when I step at last from the car and see none other than Ted stroll across the long, curved road with its order of bare trees. His wife is with him; then I see the rest, row upon row of them: truly, the King has visited with all his pack of attendant cards.

How can so many people squeeze into my sitting-room? I offer Laphroaig, and as always stumble over the pronunciation of the malt's exotic name. 'Your translation!' Ted says, smiling across at me. I go to the basement in search of glasses. And here, the final shot in the misfiring evening, is an angry Marjorie, whom we have already woken. I shouldn't have brought this crowd back home at past midnight. They must go. There are, as schoolmasters say, no ifs and buts about it.

I shan't forget the polite surprise of the strangers, all good-natured, who are now ushered from my sitting-room and my house. I can't look Ted's wife in the eye, I stand shamefaced on my own threshold; I have offered the most dastardly hospitality of all and she is doubtless glad to find it is now flouting all the rules and is annulled.

'We did harm,' Ted says this morning, when he rings. And this flings the harm back to me, in turn: what is the tone of his voice? There is not pleasure there, certainly, this is not a *Liaisons dangereuses* exercise, a spouse or lover brought low for the fun of it.

But I feel again that I am in Hell, or going there rapidly. Why is he so matter-of-fact about 'doing harm' to those he loves? And isn't it all my fault anyway?

Night. I'm sitting looking out at Notting Hill – at all the people who make up this republic of drugs, SF writers, black children on their way to Portobello

Road, Czech and Hungarian refugees from the atrocities of Hitler, staid matrons, themselves daughters of staid wardens of Oxbridge colleges, dustmen and superannuated debutantes newly arrived in the area.

It occurs to me that I'm looking at humanity – that I'm very aware of there being such an entity right now – and that, possibly, I have been excluded from it somehow. No longer a member of the human race. These banalities cross my mind as I stare out, depressed and waiting for another summons to the magnetic presence of Ted.

I might as well admit it: now I know I'm capable of delivering body blows to another woman (however much I remind myself that Ted engineered last night, kept me the place at table, seemed unable to resist bringing everyone back here afterwards I am as responsible as he.) Am I inviting more 'mayhem' just for the sake of it?

The answer to this cannot be Yes, but I sense, dimly, that my desire – I was going to write 'burning desire', so obsessed have I become with the bonfire dream, the sure psychic knowledge that something is concealed from everyone and that I, if I am to be important to Ted, should be in on the secret – my desire to learn what 'really happened' in the past has obliterated even the rudiments of good behaviour.

Bruce Chatwin's Trash

'So I said to Mrs Mandelstam, "What would you like
me to send you?" My dear, I do so love it, don't you?
– "Trash!" she said, "I want only Trash!"' And Bruce's
face goes bright pink with the pleasure of the
remembered visit to the widow of the famous poet.
His eyes, round as marbles today, roll in his head.
He has come to talk about writing for *Bananas*, and
he is in the ground-floor room of my house, the
room I try to pretend is comfortable to sit in, but
people come and strew fag ends – and, in the case
of Heathcote, apricot kernels considered good for all
manner of ailments. Bruce strides through the
detritus as if on a temporary visit – as he almost
certainly is: South America, Tibet? His feet seem to
sing out, as he paces the cheap cord carpet laid
down when I moved here. His eyes firmly refuse to
register the pathetic water-colours and odd
lithograph hanging on the wall. With his own spatial
sense – and it is one that must be obeyed – Chatwin
turns every corner of even the dingiest London
house into a potential work by a Russian Formalist
painter. 'So I made up a parcel,' he goes on. 'Agatha
Christie, that kind of thing – the trash Nadezhda
wants, in her *ghastly* life in Moscow. By the way,
George Steiner *loves In Patagonia*.' 'Oh good,' I say.

'And my mother *loves* your book,' Bruce adds kindly.

An Evening with Joseph Brodsky

It's still dark in the evenings, it feels as if winter will never end, and I think of Russia and the long nights, the cold of life in 'one and a half' rooms as described by Joseph Brodsky, in Leningrad with his mother and father when he was young. What a great distance this poet of genius has come – expelled from the USSR and now a naturalised American, he can speak and write like a native (apart from the accent) – in English – already. Brodsky is a protégé of Stephen Spender, but it was at a party in Bayswater that I met him – urged by Ted Hughes he had already given a poem to the magazine – and he greeted me with his drawling 'Wohhl', his rendition of the English 'Well', which precedes everything he says.

'Wohhl' is his reply to my suggestion that he come back with me to Notting Hill for a late drink. The party, full of self-approving literary types, clearly pleases him as little as it cheers me, even if he is the Lion for the *TLS* and *Spectator* crowd gathered here to meet him. It seems to appeal to Joseph, the idea of escaping the polite, low hum of those discussing the latest biography, or tight-lipped, finely written confessions. He hasn't heard

of our writers of realism – those writers discussed
in *Bananas* by Martin Seymour-Smith in his analysis
of English literary life in his article 'A Climate of
Warm Indifference'. Brodsky is above and beyond
the tiny world on offer in the type of English
writing admired and reviewed – still and probably
for ever – by the British Literary Establishment. I
sense that he would rather talk about poetry or
other poets than hear more of the post-war
figures – Connolly, Quennell, even the biographers
of great Victorians who still dominate these
conversations.

We go back to Notting Hill by taxi, through
black streets (it must be later than I thought). But,
as I discover, it's never too late for Brodsky to drink,
and I sit opposite him in the Elgin Crescent sitting-
room – this, as I reflect, probably more than the size
of the one and a half rooms in which he and his
family had to live. Joseph spurns my offer of vodka
(Caroline Blackwood has already told me he won't
touch Stolichnaya, he'll only drink Polish vodka, but
a Russian one is all I have. I suppose there's an
obvious reason). He settles instead on vast
quantities of whisky. Luckily I had some malt on
hand. 'Wohl, when I am in a car in the States, you
know . . . ' In the dim light of my shabby sitting-
room Brodsky looks more than ever like a
fisherman of the Black Sea coast: sandy, pale-
eyed. 'When I am on the road, I am thinking of

Wystan – of Wystan all the time – as if he was a girl, wohhl . . . '

It takes me a second or two to realise that Joseph is talking of Auden, and his obsession with the dead poet. I take a gulp of my own whisky, and I'm transported from Russia, the country to which he can never return, where I imagine Brodsky, to a road movie in what Philip Roth, calling out of the blue a while back, refers to as the US of A. (As do many, I know; somehow, seeing Joseph in the road movie he has produced for me, I can't help thinking of Auden's life in America, of Brodsky speeding down a highway, and loud Dylan on the soundtrack.) 'You think I am *sick*?' says Joseph, his grasp of the American meaning of the word in the less than a year he has been a citizen of the US as usual impeccable. 'Wohhl, perhaps I *am* sick.'

The night wears on, Brodsky talks of his son, left behind in Russia, and then of Auden again. Finally I call him a taxi. It seems darker than ever when he steps, his hundredth cigarette clamped in his lips, down onto the pavement and into the cab.

Who is Sylvia, What is She?

There's been so much to do with the magazine, and with the new book I'm writing, that the now-customary long silence from Ted has only fuelled my imagination, as if the messages he sends go straight into my work. Nevertheless, I'm still convinced he'll tell me everything one day, and I've been piecing together all I can on the one subject Ted Hughes will never talk about: Sylvia Plath.

I know there's an embargo on her being mentioned – though, bizarrely, Ted's sister Olwyn talks about her in tones of frank exasperation, as if Sylvia were still alive and causing maximum sister-in-law trouble. I suppose this is true, as death has made her immortal – but it must be due to the fact I'd just been reading the collection of her prose, *Johnny Panic*, the 'Bible of Dreams' just issued by the Plath Estate, that I found myself blundering into the forbidden chamber as soon as I saw him again.

We're driving out to Chiswick, it's a fine day and there is talk of those poets Ted most admires – Seamus Heaney, Joseph Brodsky and Eastern Europeans such as Zbigniew Herbert and Pilinszky, whose bright, jewel-sharp lines have been brilliantly translated by Hughes, introducing a readership the poets could never have dreamed of before they were picked for prominence by a major figure on the poetry scene. I keep thinking this is Ted's 'good fame' as opposed to the 'evil' one which is also forecast for him: thousands of aspiring writers have reason to be grateful to him, and students who need a window onto a wider world than the very English cadences a Philip Larkin or a John Betjeman can supply. Ted is the one who has helped novelists, too, at a time when Latin American and Slavonic writers are only just beginning to be available here. If a whole new audience has grown up for Bulgakov, or for Gabriel Garcia Marquez, Ted is one of those we must thank.

'What are you thinking?' Ted asks me as the little car whips onto the Westway (he has just announced it would be more fun to go towards Oxford than to Chiswick House or Kew).

I reply that, for someone so imbued with foreign poetry and prose, I wonder he doesn't feel like leaving England, just now going through its most parochial, whingeing and self-hating phase since the loss of Empire. 'Wouldn't you be happier' – my mind roams the wild spaces I know he likes – 'in Chile or Argentina, or somewhere?'

Ted snorts, shakes his head. He has told me in the past that he has Spanish blood, explaining his and his sister's unusually striking appearance – but now, stealing a glance at him sideways, I see a Yorkshireman, stubborn, cleft-chinned, with wily eyes and a jaw like iron. 'If I left England,' Ted says, and chooses the most melodious of his many tones of voice to deliver the punchline, 'I have the feeling England would collapse. We're a little tribe here, you know, with the Queen looking after us. Where would I go?'

I find it hard to believe that a man so reviled – for almost every review of his narrative poem

Gaudete was bitingly cruel, as transparent in its
dislike of the poet and his magical, sometimes
Satanist beliefs as of the metre and expression of the
poetry itself – can think the country would collapse
if he left it. But of course I cannot say anything like
this so I'm silent, enjoying the green grass on the
side of the road, and trees that would look suburban
and pathetic if it were not for the life everything
seems to hold when in his presence.

I think, too, that some of the hatred is personal
in quite another way: the suicide of Sylvia Plath has
turned the entire 'tribe' against her husband. Details
of the other tragic deaths – of Assia Wevill and her
child – have done little to improve his reputation.
Something in Ted, however, believes himself
indispensable to the nation. It's all very odd indeed.

'What are you writing?' Ted asks. He has
picked up some of my thoughts perhaps, on words
and magic realism and on his own unflinching way
of showing the reality of pain, in a painful world.
Yet he hasn't read my thoughts on the disasters of
the women he loved, I believe – for the car swerves
angrily as I give my answer.

'I'm . . . I'm trying to find out about Sylvia,' I
blurt out. 'Who is Sylvia, What is She?' I go on,
hardly able to understand that this self-conscious
and tactless nonsense is coming from my lips. *Of
course* I want to know about Sylvia, I long to add,
and I want to know who she was. Why aren't I

allowed to bring her into any conversation? But all of that goes unsaid, and the car slows, nosing towards an exit, a side road to take us away from the West and back into London.

'Don't talk about Sylvia,' Ted says.

We're in the park near where I live. No more than an hour has passed since my *faux pas* on the motorway. But a climate so cold and distant has descended on us both that we might have driven North, and be magically in Lapland or in the frozen tundra where Ted is really most at home, fishing by pale green lakes and making himself invisible, the better to catch his prey. It's hard to think it's the same day as when we set out, that the same sun shines on the woodland that is Holland Park's domain. Squirrels run along the branches and children walk very well-behaved with nannies or parents: there is no wildness here, except in Ted's fast, arm-swinging stride. An avenue of chestnuts is withered by his furious stare and a pond, over-full with ducks, is deprived of brackish water by his brief contempt.

Then we see it. Trotting from the little dirt path that leads into the park's heartland – led on a chain and with an expression of knowing and a total lack of fear – is a baby fox. The owner, a child of about eight years, is with her mother and – probably – her boyfriend, for the couple don't look married, somehow. They look happy, perhaps that's the reason: the fox is no bother to them, clearly, and they treat it as they would any other pet. The child beams with satisfaction. This must be, I think with a surprising twinge of envy, what she has always wanted: a fox.

'Did you know I nearly brought you one up from Devonshire the other day?' Ted says. His whole mood has altered, he is staring as if hypnotised at the animal. I in turn stare up at him, all kinds of restrictions filling my mind at the very idea of a fox brought to my house, the excitement of the children, the inevitable domestic rows and ensuing confusion. 'I should have brought it,' he goes on, and his eyes cloud as the cheerful family-with-fox party makes its way down to the Chestnut Walk. 'I nearly – there was a man selling fox cubs by the Underground – took one home to Sylvia. If I'd . . .' Then Ted's voice goes quiet, he frowns, and he doesn't seem to remember that it is I he had just wanted to appoint the guardian of a fox.

But Ted has spoken of her. All I now truly know about them, apart from gossip and American biographies which concentrate on the martyrdom of Sylvia Plath, is that he was going to buy a fox to bring home to her – and then he didn't. I know I can never ask why.

The mood stays different, light and full of promise and hope. I'm vain and pleased with myself. Like Sylvia, I deserve the present of the creature Ted most respects – almost reveres, if his famous poem 'The Thought Fox' can be said to reveal the deep feeling for the animal that he has.

I am dimly aware, nevertheless, that it is wrong of me to think too obsessively of Plath, her life and her suffering, and her marriage to this strangest of men. I want and don't want to be compared to her. I remind myself that what I don't wish for is a repetition of her jealousy and grief – though something tells me, even then in the park, that a minor version of this is what's coming my way.

It seems Ted really is serious about our trip and possible extended stay in Scotland. Talking about it today as we sit in the basement of the Portobello Hotel, all other lunchers gone and Ted's afternoon at the National Theatre cancelled with a casually arrogant phone-call to some big shot there – 'I'm under a few bottles. Can we make it another day?'! – I can't help wondering where my own will on the matter has gone.

I have become 'Scotland': I see much more clearly now, in our country that is this little 'tribe' reigned over by a monarch and held together by the strong poems Ted writes, that those women he loves or wants come to represent the countries from which they hail. Like early Shakespeare history

plays where Gloucester and York group around or
against the throne, Ted's present wife, whose father
is a farmer there, is Devon, Sylvia Plath was
America and I, coming from the one land he says
he really wants to get to know, am an amalgam of
river, salmon, heather and moor. Despite the fact I
am none of these things, I shall be for ever
Scotland.

'There's a poem by Burns,' Ted is saying, 'As I
came over Windy Gap' – 'well, it's Burns meeting an
old woman there at Windy Gap,' and Ted with one of
his magical gestures sketches in a landscape I know
so well: a stone dyke against the sky, a flinty path,
moorland going off to the line where sky meets hill.
'The old woman says to him, "Your best days are yet
to come".'

Ted looks at me intensely as he says this. I feel
what shreds of will I have left desert me. Of course I
can't just go off to Scotland, abandoning family and
home here. Whether Ted can or not, I feel resentful
when not with him that he never questions my
desire to be his companion, fellow writer, muse.
And not only my desire but my ability to leave
everyone in the lurch and take off just like that –
not in question either. I wonder about some of the
other women – Russia, perhaps, or simple suburban
Kent. Were they willing to leave with him just as
soon as he gave the word? Maybe this is what Ted
expects of the women he meets, that they will

transport him to their country and he will be
reborn, feeling new sensations, finding new words
to set them down.

But it's impossible to attack him for any of this.
Just now, he bursts out laughing and says: 'It's
Yeats, it's not Burns! "As I came over Windy Gap . . .
I am running to Paradise . . ."'

'I like the old woman at the hole in the wall
best,' I say.

'Yes,' Ted agrees. 'And it's in Scotland that I see
her – that's why I thought of Burns. So we'll put her
there, shall we?'

I'm being pulled in two directions, for today,
the first time I've really believed in this future in
Scotland, it's becoming harder and harder to know
what to do. There's something touching – and of
course flattering – about being portrayed as the
person who will provide his 'best years'. Yet . . .
somehow I know I can't do it, I just can't. Paradise
must not be the place I'm running to.

'Come back to my frosty flat,' Ted says.

Warnings, as I'm learning from the supreme
master of premonition and catastrophe, appear
often when happiness appears to have come to stay.
We're sitting in the car, on the way to the grim
traffic-choked road where Ted maintains his secret
eyrie. We pass the mansion block where I
remember being told, the first time I was taken up
to North London by him, that a 'pretty woman of

forty' had lived – and then died. I know I've already brought up the subject of Sylvia today – why do I have to ask about this woman? But, once more, like a Bluebeard's bride, it appears, I have to know. 'She died of cancer,' Ted says. Then he utters the unsayable: 'All the women I have anything to do with seem to die.'

I mustn't think of this as a warning. I daren't ask whether he thinks – as he well may – that the grisly ends of his loves are dictated from the grave by the first woman he truly loved and then betrayed. Too melodramatic. I bite my lip and look down.

We drive on, Ted talking again of Robert Lowell and his abandonment of his marriage for Caroline Blackwood – 'like a creature pulled out of the sea'. Poetic and yearning: it's clear he has fantasised this union between the great American poet and the witty, acerbic writer as a meeting of talents and intelligence such as he found once – with Sylvia.

'Doesn't she come from Ireland?' Ted says.

Today Ted's flat is piled even higher with pages of manuscript and ancient books propped open with chewed pencils, and torn paper lying thick on the ground like a kidnapper's den. I'm astonished and impressed, as so often before, by this man who, like Coleridge, never seems to stop writing – poems, plays and operas and stories for children. But even Coleridge, with his laudanum-assisted nightmares, can never have been so plain frightening as Hughes. I sit down and start to read 'The Head', his story for the magazine, and for the first time in my life I literally feel my blood run cold, as I follow the rolling, grisly head to its last resting-place, buried in the murderous psyche of a hunter. If anything, the story is reminiscent of Flaubert's 'Legend of St Julian the Hospitaller' in his *Trois contes*, with its moral of a man reared to kill, who, as he walks through a forest, is converted, by the end of the trail, to a saint, a ferryman of souls.

For all that, I look nervously to see how Ted's story ends. He has told me he believes that what he writes is only too likely to come true. In the past, he ran over a hare, only to find the death of the animal preceded the self-immolation of his wife. What will 'The Head' prophesy? But Ted doesn't want me to read the last lines here. These show the hunter accidentally and fatally wounding a soft and perfectly shaped female body in the undergrowth. When it miraculously comes to life he marries it, silent and illiterate though it will always be – and, as the punchline explaining the 'very strange wife I have' dances up before my eyes, Ted seizes the pages from me and suggests we go out for a drink.

The story is devastating and disturbing, and brilliantly written. Ted can write prose as powerful as his poetry – but does he always know what it says?

There's something triumphant about Ted when
sexual conquests – and death, whether suicide or
murder – inexplicably and chillingly become the
subject of conversation. It's disturbing; stranger still,
I find myself dredging up words thought long
forgotten, to match his snatches of ballad or rhyme.
'Who killed Cock Robin?' laughs Ted, as we drive
from Tufnell Park to Hampstead. And then, from his
own poem, 'I did it, I', followed by the great boom of
laughter that has people staring from their cars, as if
caught in a sudden thunderstorm. He is a hunter –
yet I hate hunting, and its pathological need to
show supremacy over animals witnessed through-
out my childhood when men reared to kill went out
ritually to slaughter birds reared to be killed.

　　Is it the violent end that appeals to Ted so
much? Do women, all those women who 'seem to
die' when they have known this poet/shaman,
count as little more than beasts, to him? It's
impossible not to think again of Plath's most
terrifying, angry and magically inspired poem 'The
Rabbit Catcher' and to sense she was right in
observing how the 'little deaths' excited him.
Nothing, however, can explain my own apparent
eagerness – unless my early years trying to impress
the sportsmen of the family accounts for it – to join
in Ted's bloodthirsty declamations.

We stop near the High Street and enter an unwelcoming, stripped-pine restaurant where Ted says they have good Italian food. No-one here: a feeling of the Fifties, when a trattoria was the new thing, congealed pasta and depressing salad, tired as the leatherette banquettes and chianti bottles. Ted orders a fish: it must be obvious to him that it will come from the deep freeze and not a river, but he appears oblivious of all the signals of bad food and less care. It's as if he stayed at Cambridge, in some departments at least, all his life. It's 1956; even the grey weather outside seems to announce it.

'Tweed said to Till,' says Ted when he has ordered salmon and been unconvincingly assured it is absolutely fresh, 'What gars ye rin sae still?'

'Says Till to Tweed,' I answer obligingly, 'Though ye rin with speed/And I rin slaw/Where ye droon one man/I droon twa'.'

It's macabre, Ted loves it so, and my own unexpected recapture of the lines from a Border poem learnt in youth by the River Yarrow gives him the surge of life and energy he needs – along with the subject of death, grisly and inevitable, corpses which his power of imagination makes me see along with him, floating in the wide river that was the background for so many blood-stained Border ballads.

'When I'm back from . . . ' Ted doesn't like to talk of his commitments any more than he speaks of his family. 'When I'm back from somewhere I have to go next week, we'll go to Scotland.'

Today, I decide, Ted is like a boulder on the side of a great river, unmoving, dark and impossible to reach. To argue – to try and touch this mass of stone – would be to suffer pain.

I say nothing, and watch the arrival of my gnocchi, stuck to the dish on which it has been reheated, and his salmon – which, miraculously, is indeed absolutely fresh. With the silence of deep concentration, Ted fillets the fish, then pronounces it a 'salmon trout – usually better at this time of year than the salmon', and takes the delicate spine between finger and thumb before depositing it on a plate. 'The Hebrides will be the only part of Scotland that can match up to Galway,' Ted says as he begins to eat and I sit, feeling that my own backbone has been removed, staring at the pale-pink flesh of the fish and thinking of the River Tweed near where I grew up.

'I have to give a party for the magazine,' I say, knowing how feeble this sounds. 'Will you come?'

Ted looks up, and for a moment I think he's going to burst out laughing again, at the sheer frivolity of talk about a party, when the black seas and overcast skies of the Hebrides could bring new poetry from the stormy depths. Then he decides, as I so frequently do, to say nothing at all.

'I love you,' Ted finally says.

* * *

My first-floor room in Elgin Crescent has already ingested the grins, conversations and sheepish glances of about twenty-five writers and poets when Ted arrives – and as always, when he enters a room, a silence falls. Then chatter follows; someone drops a glass of wine, I say it doesn't matter (though it does, on the soft grey carpet I put in here when I came) and I go through into the little bathroom off my bedroom for a cloth, to mop up the dark stain.

Why is it, I wonder as I come back into the room where the party is trying even harder to be a party, doorbell ringing downstairs, someone drunk already, falling on the sofa, giggling – why is it that when Ted is around nothing *does* matter? I am only pretending to dab at the marks of Beaujolais or Italian red because one of the women guests here made a fuss about the accident and tried to insist she would go downstairs to the kitchen for bucket and water, while others called for salt. I'm faking it – in reality I can feel the powerful presence of Ted over by the door, as if his book, *The Practise of Magic*, has indeed instilled the necessary methods for remote control. I come up from my knees, as red in the face, I know, as the vinous mark I was trying to remove. I look over to the door.

A girl – a young woman – she is certainly young, and what might be described as 'bouncy', is standing next to Ted. She is clinging on to his arm. Her complexion is bright and rosy and her hair is curly and dark. To make matters even clearer, she goes up on the tips of her toes as I stand marooned in the crowed, gazing at her, and kisses him on the side of the neck. The surprise – or so it seems, the sheer boldness – of such a move on arriving in the room causes Ted to laugh. Then he looks back at me. His smile is lupine, taunting.

'She's Australian,' Ian Hamilton tells me in a low voice. 'She came over after Ted last year when he'd been at the Adelaide Festival and they'd started up an affair there.'

'Last year,' I repeat, knowing I look and sound like someone in a film who has been told bad news. My voice is dull. The mirror shows the blush has drained from my face and it is blotchy and pale.

'I can see what he sees in her,' a woman someone has brought to the party (a member of what is referred to as the 'Hughes circus' perhaps) reassures me, if tactlessly.

I go back to the party. More drink is poured. Something makes me avoid Ted at all costs – I can't bear his air of triumph, nor can I pretend I can 'see what he sees in her'– Sally – as I discover she is called – is prancing round the party, showing costume jewellery which she apparently has a franchise to sell. I can't help laughing at the politely struggling refusals the guests make at the offer of the stuff. And the embarrassed expressions on their faces stay with me for hours after the party is over, as does the reluctantly granted information from too many sources to be untrue that Ted has been with Sally whenever he comes up to London. 'She's ecstatic, thinks she's Sylvia Plath,' says a friend's voice which will linger in my memory. 'His wife saw you at that party with him the other day and she thinks he comes up to be with *you*.'

Memorial Service for Robert Lowell

Church in Redcliffe Square cold and dank, British literary establishment much the same, with the wives of literary editors in moth-eaten black coats and untrimmed hair of poets straggling over collars. Honking nose-blowing, loud whispering: 'That's Caroline's mother, coming in now.'

Certainly, the arrival of Maureen, Marchioness of Dufferin and Ava, changed the scene from the thoughtful occasion this had promised to be, into a pantomime – or masque, as set before a noble audience in the days of Queen Elizabeth. Whispering grew to an astonished murmur. The flashing blue Guinness eyes, reflected, from a front pew, in the aquamarine gaze of Desmond, son of Lord Moyne and of Diana Mosley, stared out at the congregation. Diamonds much in evidence, black lace galore.

I feel the waves of Caroline's dread of her mother, from way back in the church, and for a moment I consider creeping to a front pew. But there are too many Guinnesses there: Jonathan, brother of Desmond, elder son of Diana Mitford who married the Fascist leader Oswald Mosley from the home of Joseph Goebbels; the young Lindy Dufferin; Caroline's brother Sheridan who is her husband; then another mermaid, drowned eyes like Caroline's: Doune Plunkett, living, as I was some months ago informed was my destiny, on a remote island in the Hebrides.

Ted is here, of course, but I don't see him until it's nearly time for him to stand and declaim, for he's sitting in a row of poets, in front too but on the other side of the aisle. Then, before he goes to take his stand, he sees me and strolls down, to take up a position in the pew behind me. My friend Peter Eyre, who has come with me through the crowds of Earl's Court, shrinks back and pretends tactfully that no-one has come in behind us. This is hardly the moment for introductions.

'I've been thinking about you.' Ted's face is close to mine; he seems to be half kneeling, half sitting and the tone of his voice, an answering tone, sounds as if he replies to questions from a catechism. As usual, whether I have missed *him* or not is neither here nor there. It's impossible not to think of the women who must have had to wait while Ted conducts these tests: if a certain time elapses, a month or two, say, in which he discovers he hasn't given a thought to them, is the affair definitely over? Yet, as so often with Ted, there is a cruel logic. If you don't think about someone, surely you can't be very concerned whether you see them or not.

The organ music changes, the congregation rustles in expectation. 'It's time,' Ted says – but he shows, with a meaningful look, that he means it's time for us to get together, on a more established basis. I feel the colour rise in my cheeks as he walks back down the aisle and rejoins the other readers at the service. Peter, possibly acting the part of demure duenna, sits with religiously half-closed eyes beside me.

Watching the service, I find my eyes are fastened – as she intended, no doubt, for there is nothing she loves more than an audience – on the lacy, sparkling figure of Maureen Dufferin. I hear Lowell's poems, spoken by Ted and by a host of other, lesser poets, I sing hymns and I kneel and rise. The church heats up and smells of damp wool and candles. Yet I find the resentment I've felt at Ted's absences after bringing the Australian girl, Sally, to my party some months back is melting, as I try to concentrate on the ceremony. I'm under his spell again, I can feel my face change and my own sense of dread creep in with quick panic stabs.

It's a good time now since I last saw Ted, and I'd worked out to my own satisfaction the unconscious necessity on his part to replay the

tragic sequence from his first marriage – down to
the flaunting of the new dark-haired mistress and
the obvious distaste for domesticity. I'm unable in
the church to resist replaying the last occasion we
were together – in a fish restaurant, a cheap one
this time, Geale's in Notting Hill Gate, and his quick
assurances of his inability to become a part of my
life.

'I can't change nappies,' Ted said. It was clear
that this wasn't a failure of skills which he regretted:
he was saying he can't and won't; and yet I've not
asked him to do this, nor – if he had taken the
trouble to find out – do I have a child young enough
to need them.

We ate in silence. The batter was a mistake,
despite the freshness of the fish. It occurred to me
that, for all the rough simplicity he exudes, Ted
really does like expensive restaurants, soft lighting
and the rest. Geale's has pensioners in knitted hats
taking a cup of tea alongside eaters of fish and
chips.

'I hesitate to ask you to my frosty flat,' Ted said
as a cup of undistinguished coffee is plonked down
before us.

And that – or so it appeared – was that. The
dark-haired mistress had taken him over: 'Australia'
had won. ('At least,' said Arnold Feinstein, scientist
husband of the poet Elaine, as he drives us
erratically away from a Notting Hill party in the

week of Ted's public introduction of Sally to us all,
'At least she has youth on her side.') It was the first
time, I believe, I felt truly old. A shiver of
apprehension rocked me, when I thought of that
'pretty woman of forty', and how she had gone on to
die. Would this, too, happen to me?

The party in Caroline's vast flat at the top of
the Redcliffe Square house is empty at first – why
do I walk so quickly away when it is good manners
to wait until it's time to go? Why do I walk into
Caroline's bedroom, once the maid hired for the
evening has let me in? I'm in a fog – but a glance in
the mirror satisfies my curiosity. I had to see if it
was true, for like Ted I seem to have come to believe
in all the superstitions and occult practices on
earth. My face *has* changed. I must want to be
here when he arrives, walking from the gloomy
church through winter darkness to the house on the
corner where Caroline and Lowell were happy and
then unhappy, until at last he had to make his final
flight, to America.

It takes the entrance of Caroline into her own
bedroom to jolt me from the narcissistic trance I've
been enjoying. 'Christ!' she mutters, not seeing me
as she goes to collapse on the bed, to gather
strength before the reception, the champagne (since
Lowell's death Caroline drinks nothing else), the
Guinnesses and the poets all together. Then her
daughters, all three, come in too, and they are a pile

of womanflesh on the bed, sobbing, squeezing,
black hair meshing and black and brown eyes
running with mascara – Caroline amongst them like
a creature from another species, a dolphin, as
Lowell saw her, or, as Ted likes to say, a creature
pulled out of the sea. I go quietly, unseen by this
writhing, female bed of grief.

The party is lit with candles, like the church.
The poets I know kiss me and I keep away from the
Guinnesses, just as the Guinness family stay a good
distance from me. (Are our families thought to be
too alike? The 'madness', the profligate spending of
money? I don't know, but tonight I have less reason
than ever to want to be with them.)

Ted is with me, smiling. 'I'll see you tomorrow,'
he says, and he quotes, '"As I came over Windy
Gap" . . . We'll make our plan to go to Scotland.'

The Waiting Room – A Worse Chamber

Ted rings and invites me to Sally's rented flat in
South Kensington – another Australian will be there,
'a girlfriend of Sally's, Nicola', a name he
pronounces with a droll care, as if the vowels and
consonants need to be divorced from each other
before he can permit them to roll off his tongue. He
gives directions: it's one of the gloomy mansion
blocks you find off Gloucester Road, haunt of
Australians.

I'm surprised, I have to admit, and not a little relieved by this invitation. For I know now, whether I am 'Scotland' or not, I cannot go there with Ted. I've dreamt of water, a boathouse where a woman with long straight black hair comes in close as I sleep and stares intensely down at me. I know the dream is about jealousy; I can't provoke it so wantonly; besides, I have no desire to leave my own domestic set-up, so seldom acknowledged by him.

I can't go; but the sight which greets me when I walk up to the second floor flat in Elvaston Place made me wonder at him asking me there so soon after the Lowell memorial service and its attendant passionate demand I go and live with him in the Hebrides. The drama being played out now has become cruder, almost garish in its clear intention to shock and disturb me: I would be unsurprised to hear the news of my approaching end, and then the drums Ted tells me he loves to play when inspiration and diabolical rejoicing are under way.

The flat opens onto a dark corridor with several doors off it and what is obviously the sitting-room at the end. A young woman with a bony face and freckles – Nicola, I suppose – gliding in a caftan-like garment, comes to let me in. She turns on her heel so fast I get the feeling she wants me to follow at a slower pace, and I do. There is a smell of fish cooking in an oven, a smell of singed scales and flesh. I blink in order to see more clearly: is Ted in

the kitchen perhaps, tending a sea bass, his
favourite fish? Is the kitchen through one of these
doors, and if so which?

Sally stands in the doorway of the door I push
ajar; she is giggling, triumphant and wears a wrap
half-pulled against her body. I'm closer to her than I
allowed myself to be when she came to the party,
and I see a wide face, eyes set aslant, grey-blue in a
freckled expanse of once-tanned skin. She moves
towards me as if to perform a clumsy embrace, and
the bed behind her is revealed to my gaze: sheets
rumpled and pillows scattered. A kind of sighing
laugh sounds behind me. Nicola must have retraced
her route down the darkened passage. There is no
sign of Ted.

'He's fussing with the sea bass,' Nicola says, as
Sally makes a mock-pout and congratulates me on
'the tan on my arms'. I step backwards, find the door
and walk down to the sitting-room. Here, a dismal
room with ugly flowered chintz sofas and a
selection of the costume jewellery Sally sells lying
on bamboo coffee tables. Walls a nicotine-stained
magnolia, empty bottles of Riesling on the floor by
an equally rumpled sofa. Ted comes in – the kitchen
turns out to be just off this room – and the fish stink
wafts in after him. 'Been in hours and it won't cook,'
he says as Sally, now in jeans and a plunging black
nylon jersey top, swaggers – there is no other word
for it – into the room. Aha! her stride and the tilt of

her head and dancing curly mop of dark brown hair announce to the world. Like the anchor with which the poet liked to adorn his name in his inscription of the sinister manual of magic to me, Sally goes to him and drags heavily against him. An anchor – but this one, unlike the domestic weight Ted likes to represent as his duty to his wife and home, is, as Sally wishes to make clear, fantastic, antipodean sex. Ted is tied down for the evening, and beyond.

I watch these proceedings, seeing myself standing upright in my turquoise-green silk dress with little star and moon shapes in bright colours swaying on the pleated length, and my legs in shoes too prone to turn underfoot. Nicola walks round the room with a strained smile – maybe she's in a good mood, maybe she knows better than I do what will happen next. 'It's raw,' Ted says with his great laugh, waving to the bass that lies behind a glass oven door, stubborn even when removed from silver foil, weighty and dense and clearly uncooked. It's also clear he hasn't seen Nicola yet: 'Hello there!' booms Ted, a brawny arm extruding from a rolled-up shirtsleeve, a perfect impersonation of a sheep-station manager, a man freed from the constraints of English literature – and, for that matter, marriage and responsibility as well. To Sally, next: 'Where's the champagne?'

It's only after an hour or so of Sally and

Nicola's conversation, random but power-filled, as if
to remind me of their ownership of this unusual
conquest, this 'celebrity' known, if not in England,
as the husband of Sylvia Plath, and the architect of
her suicide, that I realise we are not going to eat.
Also, as Ted rises and pulls on a jacket, that he is
no-one's possession; that his greatest pride is, like
the salmon he worships, leaping upstream,
outwitting nature, dodging human snares and baits
as well. 'I'll take you home,' Ted says to me. 'And
drop me off,' Nicola says, as a quick look passes
between them. 'I won't be long,' says Ted, walking to
the door.

I didn't look back. Sally, trying to render me
absurd, calls out as I walk with Nicola – we're about
the same height, we both have fairish hair and
strong features – 'The terrible two!' and Ted laughs
again, still bonhomous, as contented as if he had
consumed the fish over which he has taken so
much care. 'Don't be long!' Sally's voice is brittle,
shows a nervous edge: can he really be interested in
someone else, when he has – and has had again, so
recently – such pleasure with her? 'We'll talk about
a trip to the Caribbean,' Sally calls out as the front
door of the flat is reached and Ted pulls it open. 'I
want tanned arms too!'

But in great downward jumps, three steps at a
time, Ted has disappeared from the dominion of
Sally. I follow as fast as I can, damning the

treacherous shoes that buckle under my feet. Nicola fidgets as we reach the street, her smile growing more strained as she is forced to lose speed beside me. We find the car, and settle in like released prisoners – yet, I can't help asking myself as we head for North London, for the long car journey that will make its first stop in Shepherd's Bush and then back to Notting Hill – what was I doing there in the first place?

The basement is dark, some of the lights there aren't working, and I stumble as I try to reach the tall lamp. My foot has turned, in the evening sandal with the broken heel; I find myself marched up and down in the gloom, with street lights dimly visible by the steep steps from basement to gate into the street. The back of the long room and kitchen, where the children's doll's house looms even larger than in the Old Drawing-room at Glen, where my father made and placed it, is inky black. An owl makes ge-wick! ge-wick! out in the gardens; Ted pauses, in his swift passage with the wounded, and cocks his head the better to hear it. It occurs to me, through the throbbing pain of my ankle, that this figure almost invisible in the strange surroundings once so familiar – my own kitchen, the room where the children play – has the look of a fox, a dog fox, slightly greying, still alert to every sound from the natural world. Then my hand reaches the switch,

and the place is flooded with light; and as if my
twisted foot is a masquerade rather than the real
thing, I try to stroll casually to the leather sofa
against the wall. But the pain won't go away – and I
can sense the alarm and concern, the fear of being
near a hurt woman, coming off Ted as I hobble to sit
down.

This is where, I think as I look around –
anywhere rather than into his eyes, which are
trained away from me and my disability as if we are
strangers on a train, or in a doctor's waiting-room,
placid, inward-looking – this is where the subject of
Scotland first came up. Where we met, on the night
the Russian poet came and the declaiming of
Tsvetayeva's poem went on far into the night. Now,
where are we? Nowhere, not even in Scotland, I
reflect, with a mixture of gratitude and sadness.
How did I think we ever could be? The sprained
foot, echoing my despair and anger at myself,
intensifies the agony, and I ignore Ted, for the first
time since I've met him, and concentrate on the
pain.

'Your father made the doll's house?' Ted is
saying, when the rhythm of discomfort dies down
enough to remember I'm here, at eleven at night, on
the leather sofa with the hard steel frame and the
ancient cushions that slide away as you move on
them. Neither of us has eaten; now, after dictating
to Ted the whereabouts of the whisky, we both hold

a tumbler of the mahogany stuff, he sipping
gingerly, as if taking care in advance not to be
caught with 'an invalid' – as he described the
sufferer of a recent accident at home, correcting
himself quickly after referring to the stricken
woman victim as 'a corpse'. I'm strongly aware of
his imminent departure – there is no need for me to
reiterate that I can never come to Scotland with
him, and I don't feel that pride insists I should do
this. We are like spectators at the end of our own
particular drama. But Ted, being Ted, will always
insist there is no final curtain and we are merely
sitting through the interval. He runs his arm,
tentatively, along the back of the ill-made sofa. I
can't help seeing the bed at Sally's flat, and his arms
enclosing her amongst the scattered pillows there.
'It's just a question of waiting,' Ted says.

I don't reply. This room in this house must not
become the waiting-room my injury has made it –
waiting, in this case, not for medical attention but
for a recurring illness, that of being mesmerised by
this frightening, too-powerful man. I struggle to rise
– but of course I can't, the bad foot registers its
protest and I sink back again.

'Sally – she came over to find me, you see.
Give it a year. She'll go back there.'

For some reason, I remember Ted telling me
how his father, desperate to leave his wife in
Yorkshire after meeting a pretty nurse in London,

had gone south to find her – only to be discovered almost at once by the pursuing wife, just a few streets away from King's Cross, the station of his arrival and escape. Will Sally one day trap Ted, as his father was caught by his wife? I doubt it, for, despite his portrayal of himself as anchored and held down, Ted will always move too fast for any hunter's nets. Now he is swimming off, miles upstream – and I am counselled to wait, crafty and patient, until a new tide brings him back again. 'My foot's hurting,' I say, knowing I sound like a child.

When Ted has gone, I go and look in the book of Ted's poems where Elaine told me the other day that a description of women he had loved and then left could be found. I'm shocked, but exhilarated too, to find the terror and loathing of these lovers, and I even speculate – for Elaine assures me I'm in there (though I can't be, I know) – whether Lion Eyes is, as she suggests actually me. ('Elaine is a strange girl,' Ted said when I put it to him a few weeks back that I am one of the characters in the poem. And that was that.)

Now I read the words again. 'I went into a Worse Chamber . . . ' All women are torturers to Ted, perhaps ever since the death of his first wife, Sylvia. Anything to do with women demands a return form of torture, this I now see clearly; and the wound inflicted must imitate the knife-stab administered to an unbalanced young woman, a poet and mother, with small children and an obsession with her dead father on which he liked to play.

I shall not go into the Worse Chamber and sit waiting for him there. But I know this is easier to say than to do. One day, as sudden and silent as the fox he resembles, Ted will reappear.

Now I begin to see the pattern which Ted must establish around himself in order to exercise the power that is so essential to him.

I can only see a parallel with a Great Cat – a lion, perhaps, or a puma – which brings its prey in, swinging from its jaws, and displays it before going to hide it again for the final kill.

I have been 'shown' the first victim, quiet, dark and beautiful, a proud face, infinitely patient.

I have followed the lion to one of its lairs, where the second victim lives in innocence of her approaching extinction. And this victim, prettily dangling, has been brought to me for my approval or distaste (the latter, of course, which caused the hoped-for amusement).

Now I am left to wonder at my own blindness in this Bushman's tale of his contriving. For how have I been shown to *them*? They have been brought to my house and I have been lured to theirs – I am just as 'important' or as unnecessary as they.

Of course, this cannot be said to apply to his

marriage. But I still feel we are objects of his fancy, and don't belong to the 'real' world. I feel his paws, blunt with a murderous tenderness, on my arm as I walked or hobbled around the room.

The Farewell Party

A story, 'The Head' by Ted Hughes, along with the painful letters of the poet Marina Tsvetayeva to Boris Pasternak and Bruce's account of his meeting with Mandelstam's widow in Moscow, will surely prove an excellent last 'Russian' issue of the magazine.

This it will be, under my editorship at least. Elaine has introduced me to a young woman who would like to buy *Bananas* and edit it herself. She has some money – the magazine has none. We shall meet in a week or so and I shall give the very last party for contributors and friends. I saw a glimmer of sympathy in Angela's eye when, a couple of days ago, a few people came round to celebrate the Russian issue, just back from the printers. Bill Webb, literary editor of *The Guardian* was there, and Hiang Kee, whose drawings for Osip Mandelstam's *Journey to Armenia* he published along with the review.

'You mean it's the publication day of your book as well?' Angela asks, as Bill opens a new *TLS* and starts reading out a long review of *The Bad Sister*. 'You must never get time to sit down.'

Others more organised would I am sure be able to do both – but now I want to write with at least some of the inspiration of the East Europeans

– Bruno Schulz, for instance – and try to portray my family.

My house in Elgin Crescent fills with those who have come to celebrate – or bemoan – the sale of *Bananas* to Abigail Mozley, a bald-headed 'mature student' with money from an absent husband's Cornish tin mine. All eyes are fixed on the new proprietor of the magazine, plastic bananas on her head, flamenco frills of spotted red and white cotton trailing the steps. 'Who on *earth*,' I hear the mutter from Ian Hamilton, Keeper of the Pillars of Hercules, 'is *that*?' And Ballard wears a sardonic smile which suggests the apparition has walked from one of his stories of abandoned tourists enjoying an endless fancy dress masquerade.

But the revelry – if thus can be described the violent clash of the party – ends in death, and next day, accusation. My nephew Charlie, heroin addict, has strolled into the throng and Caroline Blackwood, still suffering from the death of Robert Lowell, has brought along her daughter Natalya – who is later that night found dead from heroin in her flat. The phone rings all day. Reports come in to the effect that my nephew is blamed – whether he did so or not – for supplying drugs at the party to Caroline's eldest daughter.

This is a terrible situation. Coming so soon after the death of Lowell, it is unspeakable for poor

Caroline. Parties are closely linked to death, this flashes through my mind and I think of Proust and of the Duchesse de Guermantes and her determination to go out to dinner despite the imminent demise of her oldest friend. What can I do, to alleviate Caroline's suffering? Nothing, of course. But the aftermath of the party, the rumours and reports that drift in from people who knew nothing of what was going on, are very distressing. Ian Hamilton, who does – I suppose one has to say 'did' – know poor little Natalya well through his close association with Lowell, says she had been, if anything, rather drunk. 'She was flushed, emotional.' But there's no point in wishing I hadn't encouraged Luisa to mix the 'champagne' cocktails quite so wildly, adding brandy and vodka in a Luisa-like way. It's as much my fault as anyone's. And after all, Charlie may have supplied Natalya with drugs – it's beginning to come out that she wasn't a total stranger to them. All the more dreadful, when I think how I met Caroline with my brother, all those years ago at Brown's when she let me come with her to the Ladies and watch her spit into her little box of mascara. For some reason, this upsets me more than anything and I cry all day, interspersed with dodging phone-calls from press and relatives of Caroline.

This is the end of *Bananas*. 'I hear it was a bad party, from Carmen,' says a friend who'd been away

and unable to come. And I think, Yes, it was a bad
party: I didn't know half the people there, a
Bananas party had just become something to crash.
The new proprietor of the magazine has serious
plans to concentrate on translated fiction and
poems, devoting a whole issue to a country and its
writers, and I wish her well. Our own mix won't be
repeated, or probably even remembered, except
when acknowledgements appear in the frontispiece
of collected stories by Angela Carter, Ted Hughes or
J. G. Ballard. So what? I say to myself, but I feel
miserable all the same, a misery it's hard to separate
from the dreadful accident. Somehow, the frivolity
of the party and the bright red and white of the new
proprietor's Carmen Miranda get-up grow into a
huge miasma – go where I may in the house or out
in the summer-deserted gardens, I can't escape it.
And I think of Caroline, sitting upstairs in her flat
and drinking. When Natalya's father died – I
remember the grief and relish of Caroline as she
recounted the grim tale. 'Natalya insisted on going
to see him. We all had to go with her. They had put
him in Harrods, you know' – and that laugh of
Caroline's, when she says it's the *worst*, so awful
there's nothing you can do but laugh. 'We nearly
fainted.'

This is such a typical story of Caroline's that,
remembering it, I go to the phone to ring her up.
But then – how can I? There's something of her

mother, the litigious Maureen, Marchioness of
Dufferin, in Caroline and she might sue – for the
party causing her daughter's death? It's impossible
to say. But the shifting around of the Guinness
millions, the endless references to lawsuits and
court cases make it too much of a risk to contact
Caroline when she's in this state of mind.

Night. Just as I was trying to tie up the magazine's
loose ends and hand over to Abigail, Ted rang and
asked me to lunch at his sister's house on Sunday.
As usual, an age has passed – but this invitation is a
new development. I shall see him in a different
light, with his children. I know they matter more
than anyone else to him, and were the reason for
his anguished – and angry – attack on the poet
Alvarez, when he unleashed some years back the
then-unknown facts of Sylvia's death. I feel –
almost – as if we have never lost touch. This
after the unending silence, demoralising and
inevitable, to which I have become so unfortunately
inured.

Lunch with Frieda and Nicholas

'Don't send Ted out for cigarettes!' Olwyn, standing
in the sitting-room of her house in Camden Town,
has today allowed the mother hen to overtake the
still-glamorous and enigmatic, slightly Juliette

Greco Left Bank appearance she often presents, if
unthinkingly, to the world. Pans are bubbling in the
kitchen at the back of the house. A smell of roasting
meat is dimly there, and onion, blackening as a
result of my late arrival. I decide to offer a helping
hand and then think better of it; I stand, aware I
shouldn't really be here at all, and thankful that
Joseph Brodsky is the other guest. Already, I regret
accepting this invitation to Sunday lunch, issued
yesterday by Ted on the phone and seeming, at
first, to suggest an important new start in our
relationship. To meet the family – to meet those
most precious to Ted – had seemed at first an
expression on his part of love and trust in the
future. Gladly abandoning my own family in order
to leap this particular gulf, I have to confess to the
indulging of the most sentimental and foolish of
fantasies: we would all be happy together, etc. etc.,
this omitting, madly, the man I actually hoped to go
on living with and Ted's present wife, whom he has
been, in the words of Elaine, 'longer with, God
knows, than anyone else'. What had I really
expected from this ill-advised encounter? All I knew
of myself, as I set out from Notting Hill in a tardy
and ill-organised dash North, was that I could
scarcely fail to give a bad impression to the
offspring of Sylvia Plath and Ted Hughes. Deciding
to wash my hair at the last minute was clearly as ill-
considered as Ted's invitation to his sister's house.

My head, surrounded by a haystack of beige frizz, was made all the less reassuring in appearance by another foolish decision, that of applying very red lipstick in order to try and establish some shape to the face buried in this uncontrollable haze. I wondered whether Ted's disappointment – my clothes were as rashly put together as the rest – hadn't accounted for his rapid suggestion he go and buy me cigarettes, this postponing at least the moment when he would have to contemplate the reaction of his family to the spectacle just arrived. I, inevitably, had left hairbrush at home, as well as the packet of Bensons for which I frantically searched after the front door was opened to me by the seventeen-year-old 'Little Frieda'. I was a mess, there's no other word for it. And Olwyn's gruff greeting, 'Don't send Ted out for cigarettes!' was hardly likely to make me feel welcome in the profoundly terrifying presence of near-grown-up children of whom one has read tragic reports in their infancy.

Nervous states, however, can provide unexpected insights, and it was Sylvia I saw when the door opened and her daughter stood there. Sylvia not exactly as the (invariably) unflattering photographs show her, but Sylvia young, fair and full of the strength and vigour she famously possessed. At the same time, the woman child who admitted me, had a deceptively settled – in itself

almost unsettling – poise. This was Sylvia pleased
with herself – and Sylvia's daughter, anxious,
doubting, as she lets a stranger into the house.

By the time I had pulled myself together – and
both Ted and his sister had come into the hall to
find me there – I was able to indicate to Ted's
daughter that I'd found her stories, sent me some
time back by her aunt, 'very good – promising . . .'
I don't know what I said, for the dreadful truth is,
and will perhaps always remain, that a first sighting
of Plath's children will bring to mind primarily and
even exclusively the tragedy that surrounded their
early years. It was as this was going through my
mind that I dug in my bag and found my cigarettes
were missing; and Ted said he'd walk to the off-
licence in the next road.

Now, as he's such an age going about it, I find
myself in the most awkward and delicate situation
– that of demonstrating, as I rapidly see I must do,
my total lack of importance in the life of the father
of these children. Yet there's no-one here to assist
me in doing so. Brodsky, who has seen me with
Ted a couple of times, gives the unfortunate
impression of having seen us regularly – mention
of 'How's Caroline?' and his and Ted's reading at
Lowell's memorial service (it's obvious Ted and I
have been close, at her flat, later), an allusion to a
recent party. And Olwyn has gone into the
kitchen.

I am intensely aware, as the minutes tick by –
and Ted finally appears (it has even occurred to me
that, like Henrietta's husband, the poet Dom
Moraes, Ted might have 'gone out for cigarettes and
never come back': he's certainly well capable of it) –
I'm aware, as I say, of a definite over-pronounced
interest in the nature of our relationship on the part
of Nicholas, Ted's son. No sooner has his father
come into the room, handed me a packet of
Rothmans – 'It's all they have' – and moved us all
into the kitchen, than a yellow Kodachrome
envelope is produced and a raft of family snapshots
is laid on the table. 'The great photographer!' says
the boy, of his (clearly much-loved) step-mother.
'Look at that one,' and so on. I am excluded; I should
never have left Back Street. I begin to long to go
home as the holiday pics – I don't want to look, but
I have to pretend an acquaintance's half-feigned
interest in the shots, some absurdly out of focus, of
a pretty dark-haired woman a good deal younger
than Ted, and sporting teenagers against a
background of grass, river and trees – spill out on
the table's surface.

Olwyn serves the lamb; Brodsky and Ted talk,
mainly about Eastern European poets of whom I
know little. Then Ted – for he can hardly have failed
to see his son's eyes trained on me with all the force
of apprehension of horror he cannot conceal, leans
across him and addresses me gravely. He speaks of

the story he is writing for the magazine. He gives a
delivery date for looking through the text – 'if we're
not abroad'. Hardly able to reply, I say late June will
be fine.

'So you're one of Dad's *editors?*' The voice,
only just breaking, goes through octaves of relief
and joy. 'You *work* together?'

The answer comes that this is indeed the case.
But, when I flee after a perfunctory cup of coffee,
and find myself in the clean, empty air of North
London caring not at all which bus may come or
whether a cab will bear me home, I feel the anguish
of the child who knows or suspects too much,
descend on me. What is most feared – infidelity,
desertion – will all be acted out again one day; and
like a puppy whining by its master's door, Ted's son
must alert all those who pass to the expected
betrayal and ensuing flight.

But the daughter – or so it seems to me, at least
– has a greater sense of herself than her brother has
of his own identity. Her father's marriage and its
future are not a major concern for her. I stand a while
down on the corner where there's enough traffic to
suggest a possible taxi, and look back once: the
house I've visited is already hidden by another low-
roofed row of 'villas'. There's no sign of the family
party, which has a plan to visit the British Museum
this afternoon: I wasn't included in the trip: indeed,
as I now know, I never could have been.

A note from Ted just over a week ago – 'I've just got through a wonderfully dense wall of obstacles just lately, and when I've got through the US, from Monday for 2 weeks, maybe I'll be clear to move. I hope you'll still be there' – and here I am indeed, only I'm heading for the garden of my childhood, and not (for once) Holland Park, with all its restrictions, fences and boundaries.

Here, driving through the open spaces of Regent's Park, I pointed out the terrace, Chester Terrace, where I grew up. 'What Number?' 'Thirteen' makes us both laugh. But I felt the onset of panic, followed by a drowsy acceptance of Ted's hypnotic powers, as we drove on, leaving a past where we could have known each other – a past he shared with a woman he tries to show me by cunning and stealth, in a mass of coded references, astrological and geographic. 'We'll go up to Chalk Farm,' Ted says, although we have been heading for his eyrie high above the thunder of the lorries bound for the North. 'Then the Heath – perhaps we'll find violets there, or a wild rose to take home.' And he adds, as if to stress the importance of the mood we must enter if we are to return to our early haunts, 'We might see each other—.' 'Like Miss Moberley who went to Versailles with her companion and sat in the garden there', I put in, 'and saw the court of Marie-Antoinette.'

'Yes.' But I know from the dismissive tone that a Petit Trianon is not what Ted hopes to see. He wants something further back in history, a parliament of birds perhaps, like the famous Persian book of that name he has given me to read. Or, truly, a glimpse of a woman he knew; a ghost; a woman he will admit one day, as Thomas Hardy did with his first wife, to be his one true love. The thought brings a familiar sense of exclusion, and I look back across the road to the rows of Nash houses, yellow as crumbling teeth in the afternoon sunshine, which encircle the sward of the park. 'I can show you a secret garden instead,' I hear myself say. And I hold back from saying, too, that this garden is where I used to go, to escape the world, fleeing even the openness of the park, when I was young. As well as escape, as I remember suddenly with the braking of the car, the swing through the gates of Regent's College, that this is the garden, off the Inner Circle and in my mind bound by all the circles of the Inferno, where a young man I had loved made it clear to me that he no longer cared for me at all. Have we loved others and worn ourselves out, Ted and I? There's an element of that, certainly: in the words in a letter from him, 'maybe I'll be clear to move. I hope you'll still be there', in the long silences and the memory of a party in Belsize Park earlier in the year at which a

stranger came up to us, thought we were a couple
(why? the way we stood, or talked?) and was put
right ferociously. It *is* too late – too late for anything
but the Blue Garden, as it is called, where blue
flowers, like sapphires planted in the earth, spill
from carefully weeded beds. I knew Ted would like
it here, and he does.

Regent's College, rigorous and symmetrical in
its beauty, is guardian of this extraordinary place. I
see – of course! – that something in the mood Ted
wishes us to be in can be found here in the wide
arms of espaliered trees set in a diadem by the
beech and nut hedges at the far end. I see the Blue
Garden grow, in his imagination, from the book I
gave him before he went to America. And now I
feel less excluded, almost alive again, and the words
that end his latest note return to me. 'Just finished
The Blind Owl. Now re-reading it. Stunned. A key to
the door – for me.'

This is the door to which Ted thinks I possess
the key: this is my secret chamber. 'My' Blue
Garden, shaped like a womb, invisible to the stern
male eye of the college of architecture once you
have walked down the wide, curving steps and
passed through the first enclosure of tall green
hedge. No-one ever comes here, nobody seems to
know. I have counted forget-me-not and borage and
the tiny speedwell in the turf. Now, because
summer has begun and the open-air theatre across

the Inner Circles resounds with Titania and her
hypnotic fantasy, I see phlox, a mauvish blue, and
the first delphiniums, royal-blue swords in their
leafy costume that is a piercing light green. 'There
just needs to be water,' Ted says, and I know he
means the opium dream in *The Blind Owl*, the book
by the Persian writer Sadegh Hedayat which
changed that country's perception of literature in
the middle of the century and now changes Ted's
view of the power of writing as it has mine. The
repetition of the dream; the lost past returned; the
endless sleep that is a waking dream; these are the
eidetic visions given by *The Blind Owl*, from a writer
who left his native country, went to Paris in the war
to study with Sartre, and killed himself there later.
But Ted doesn't talk of Hedayat's suicide, and
neither do I. A door has been opened – and I am
proud to have opened a door for one already so
possessed by Persian lore and myth.

We're in an arbour of trees that form an open
fairy ring, a band of chained prisoners, scarfed by
leaves along the wires which bind them together,
here in the most hidden part of the garden. There
are no blue flowers anywhere, for an enclosure of
high walls of box and beech makes it too dark here
for them to grow – and the grass is uncertain,
revealing bald patches of a dry-blood earth.

Ted leans down, and his hands go round my
neck, and as they tighten I am a tree, held by

metallic twine in the cruel shape ordained for this arboreal amphitheatre in the Blue Garden. I am offered up in the deep shade of the hedge, and have no more life in me than the foliage, parched from lack of light, that runs raggedly between the espaliered trees. I could die here – and float away like the last of the cherry blossom that dances over the heads of the actors in Regent's Park. But this is no play: I feel my ears sing; my eyes blur as I look up into a face that grows from the pagan roots of the trees, a Green Man killing with his bare hands in the forest's depths. Then, with no more sense of time than *The Blind Owl* visionary's dream, we have walked out of the shade together and through the garden, to our car parked alone on the forecourt of Regent's College. There are no students to be seen.

Ted Hughes Sees a Ghost

'You only get three chances,' Ted says. We're walking up a steep road in Notting Hill – from Clarendon Road to the layer of tree-lined crescent higher up where he has left his car – and I think of the 'chance' we had, suggested by him, of going to the North of Scotland – to stay? to live? to escape? I never really knew. Has the first chance already been spent, subsumed in commitments and hesitations? 'Ted is very long-distance,' his sister once said of him, with the long-drawn-out half-laugh she puts on when the name of the man who brought Sylvia and thus undreamt-of responsibilities into her life comes up. 'He doesn't see that time has gone by.'

I fall back a few steps on the abrupt climb of the road; Ted walks on, a slow, measured walk. He is carrying a fishing-rod; I can't think why, though there's something enjoyably ludicrous about imagining him in Kensington Gardens, at the Round Pond, angling for tiddlers amongst the children's sailing-boats. Only a great fish – a pike, of course – or, for the table in whatever flat he happens to be staying in, a sea bass – will do. I catch up with him and ask if he's seen that a salmon has been espied, up the Thames at Teddington. I babble on, about cleaner water and the rest – but I am still to be instructed on the Three Chances and what they mean. 'The first time,' says Ted firmly, 'it's perfect. Just right.' He stops on the hill and turns, to loom over me. 'If you fail to take it, have care with the second chance.'

'What happens then?'

'It's . . .' He stretches out his arms as if to try and catch a throw which has gone wide of the mark. 'It's tainted – something goes wrong; it's not quite right.'

I stand still. Ted has the ability literally to root his listeners to the ground. I sense an uneasy universe, presenting the second chance on a salver, then slinking away with it when it turns out to have gone bad.

'The third chance . . . ' Now there's laughter, almost angry. 'Why, it's a disaster. Don't take it. It's no good at all.'

For a moment, as a cloud goes over the sun, and a wind gets up, blowing the branches of a tree across his face, I see a figure, half-human, half stag, standing on a hill. I see the world Ted Hughes inhabits, so powerful is his projection of an imagined scene. Am I 'Scotland – the one country I need to get to know better'? Do I exist only as a divining-rod to the hidden wells of a new poetic life? I begin to wonder if this is the 'second chance', disguised as the perfect, right and unspoilt offer of the first. But a car, crawling up the hill, stops with a clumsy shifting of gears at the crossroads no-one, in this labyrinth of one-way streets, seems to cross. A radio brings in Radio Four news. We walk on.

In my sitting-room, looking out at the chopped-down tree stump through French windows that open onto an uncertain balcony. We drink a malt – a need to please, to prove how 'Scottish' I am, has led me to bring in the bottle. It comes from an island far to the North of where I grew up – a fact Ted doesn't want to accept: I'd be more romantic as a Highlander. Does he see in me a Celtic twilight that simply isn't there? Peat-brown, rich, however you say it the stuff goes down well as the afternoon draws in. An autumnal dusk hovers, and in the last light the Venetian colours of the houses opposite appear brighter than they do by day.

Ted goes to the long window and stands staring out at the street. He is silent – for so long that I must have moved restlessly on the sofa. Then he turns to me. 'You could say we know as much of what is really going on as someone who looks out to sea and suddenly catches sight of a fin . . . ' He holds up a finger, tracing the fin through an ocean which is instantly visible. 'That is all we know.'

I stare, as quiet as he had been.

'A girl – it's how she would have looked now. She was a child, Shura. Walking past. That's all.'

Black Venus

Lunch with Angela at Thompsons. Every time I
meet Angela I want to ask her to write another of
her beautiful, strange stories – but now of course
there is no magazine to put them in. I explain my
new plan, a set of spirally bound notebooks which
would each contain a tale or a sequence of poems,
and drawings or paintings as illustrations. 'Of
course,' Angela says; and as always, her whole
frame shakes with hidden laughter, as if the elves
and sprites who populate her imagination have
taken hold of her limbs and danced carelessly over
her. I strain forward, envisaging the notebooks, and
as I talk of French books in their plain paper covers
– I have a set of Baudelaire given me by my mother
when she went to live abroad – images of Paris
overwhelm Angela and she becomes more
incapable of speech than ever. 'Jeanne Duval,' she
finally manages.

I am too ignorant to know – or in any case
remember – who Jeanne Duval might be. Angela
explains, in a thousand, half-begun and then
abandoned sentences, that Duval was Baudelaire's
black mistress. 'I'll . . . I'll . . . ' Angela says. We have
a new story. I feel a surge of delight at the idea of
the little *livres de poche* which must somehow be

brought into being, to accommodate the length
needed for each imaginative venture – rather than a
length dictated by a publisher for a work of fiction.

As we sit on, in the silence filled with half-
thoughts and orchestrated by waiters bringing
moules or monkfish or, to ladies lunching with
bright, greedy eyes, the *Tarte tatin*, apples in a soft
pastry, caramelised, glistening, I see a familiar
figure rise from the gloom at the far end of the
restaurant and make his way to the door. Our table
is unavoidable, on the way out – not that Philip Roth
has any wish to look away from Angela as he comes
nearer. He bows low; Angela looks up at him in
surprise.

'I congratulate you on *The Sadeian Woman*,'
Roth says. He bows again, and pushes aside the
green velvet curtain by the door, gazing back once
and repeating the compliment in a low, intense
voice.

It's true, Angela's book of that name has just
come out, from Virago. As we sit, Angela's flaming
cheeks evincing the mixed feelings a compliment
from such a quarter must provoke, I can't help
thinking of the room the author of *My Life as a
Man* goes back to, to write of himself and his *alter
ego*. I think of the rubber mat, occupying the small
space between desk and wall. For a second a vision
of Roth as de Sade flashes across my mind. He
clearly likes Angela – but she is far too canny to

become a Rothian woman: Angela can take care of herself.

From the Demon of the Dee

Is Ted mad? A letter came from him today – an April day in the North, in the Scotland I have come to reign over, in his imagination – and I see him from far away, a rock with a million fissures, a man whose appearance of confidence and strength is belied by fears, perhaps by fears of further nervous visitations.

'The demon experimental psychologist', he writes, 'got me in his white rat testing laboratory – and the futile wheels, the whimsical electrical shocks, and switches, the vindictive images and sudden brain-wave endurance test were coming thick and fast . . . '

Before he goes on to assure me that my 'native land has moved the whole range of harassment into a whole new order of intensity' by virtue of the freezing temperatures on the River Dee, I return the letter to its small brown envelope. It's the kind of envelope that bears a bill from a country greengrocer and can hardly be expected to carry news that 'the salmon have become stone, pink granite no doubt . . . and are now busy fracturing into pebbles, with the hammering freeze-power of what bit of water there is' or, again bursting the

seams of its modest brown container, that the writer
was 'struggling – with some hope – through a vat of
cold treacle, a gasometer full of bran, and across a
vertical river on a revolving escalator'. I wonder,
not for the first time, if the agonies Ted has
undoubtedly suffered have made him a constant
prey to terrors of the 'white rat testing laboratory'
even when away with his son, as he is now, and
fishing a royal stretch of river.

How could anyone, and especially a poet to
whom each sound, animal, bird and colour spells a
new language of discovery, possibly survive the
deaths of two women and a child, the last two a
blatant imitation of the first? Does the very nature
of the second suicide explain his horror of
repetition, in itself a trembling signal of the onset
of madness? Can guilt, for this he undoubtedly
feels, drive a man actually mad? Is every cry of pain
in poem and prose a cry at the gouging of the eyes,
the playing out of a fate which – as all say who
punish and accuse him – was a fate of his own
contriving? Does Ted's 'madness' reflect a longing to
die, the obsession with death a prophylactic for the
real thing?

But of course, Ted likes to play the Fool as well
as Lear. His mouth twitches just when tragedy has
set in, at the sheer idiocy and predictability of his
fate. His letter goes on to assure me that the efforts
in the vat of cold treacle and the gasometer full of

bran were all accomplished 'with the pen in my teeth' and 'the vertical river on a revolving escalator' was crossed in vain, for he had been deprived of 'the bottle of ink'. And I can't help laughing out loud, thinking there can seldom have been so weird a set of references to the fact of my gift to him of a fountain pen. I remembered how I'd found him at the bar in Clarendon Cross, scribbling a poem on a shabby piece of paper, to try out the nib – and I saw in my mind's eye the bottle of black ink, posted to Devon and (presumably) lost before the pen could be filled. It is a familiar, cosy madness suddenly, though the threat of the white rat testing laboratory – 'So it was O Emma that I felt he'd had a visit' – remains constant, a chill undercurrent.

Now all I do, as ever, is marvel at the range of images which fly across Ted's mind, even as, as he says, his hands are getting sawn off daily with the most stunning cold and his feet numbed in freezing rivers. The physical agony may distract from the next visit of the demon psychologist. I think back to the issue of the magazine in which we published poems given us by Olwyn – I hadn't even met Ted yet – and remember his lines 'The comings get closer/The goings get worse'. Did he refer then to the mad times?

I've had a card from Ted, about my new novel, *Wild Nights*. 'I can't forget it', goes the strong, spidery handwriting. As usual, months pass before he gets in touch again, and it's just when you decide he *has* forgotten, that the call comes.

Holland Park – where else? – is where we go, but only after a visit to the Portobello Hotel, to a cabin-sized room booked by me and then paid for by me (this to show a final abnegation of responsibility for the affair? Possibly; it hurts and irritates at the time, as it may have been meant to do). So far, in our relationship, I have given Ted a pen, an expensive Mont Blanc, and he has given me books. I've heard of jewellery-buying sprees on his part – his sister Olwyn likes to say that Ted could be seen to be 'different' as a child, for he dreamt frequently of jewellery – and I know he buys trinkets for Sally as well as choosing marital gifts. Clearly, ours is a 'literary' romance. The question why I still am willing to see and meet him in this way is as unanswered as ever it was.

Today, however, there is a sense of change, of relief and sadness on Ted's part which makes him gentle, almost resigned. Apart from tales relayed by friends of his increasing boredom in Sally's company, there is now news that she has packed up and gone back to Australia. But I cannot say I feel, as we sit side by side on the bed in the tiny room overlooking a tall mimosa tree in Stanley Gardens, any real intimation of a new beginning.

The fragrant yellow blossoms give an impression, on this rare, fine March day, of a tree belonging to another country and it plunges us, at least, into another season. Seeing Ted in profile, I can't help wondering what would have happened if we'd met a decade or so earlier; as so often before, he turns out to have been thinking exactly the same thing. 'Where *were* you?' he asks, turning to me, 'Why didn't I meet you then?' – and, again as so often before, there is simply no answer.

This is a last time, I can't help acknowledging: his body, pale as a lion's pelt, is stretched out now on the too-small-for-us bed and his eyes, peaceful for once, are half closed. I think of his Bushman's Story, of the animal which stalks its victim, following the prey to unknown places that become 'known' by simple strength and determination to kill, and wonder as so often before at the restless energy which drives him to hunt and then to discard what he has brought down. A devil in me prompts me to ask (for I know I've heard on the grapevine that he has been re-reading Plath's journals and letters with a view to editing and publishing) whether he has burnt – as he once told

me she had incinerated his work, in a fit of rage –
any of the material he's read. Then, just as quickly,
the devil's voice is quiet. I've spoken only in my
mind, Ted has heard nothing. Instead, it's as if there
is no ghost of Sylvia hanging over us (as there so
often is, over him, certainly: I now see she will
remain for ever the uninvited guest, when he
pursues a woman). My fear is that, with him gone,
as he will surely be by the end of today, she will
stay with me a long time. Ted is talking in a relaxed,
amused way, of the novel, recently published, by a
friend of his, Michael Baldwin. 'It is *so* profane,' he
says, and laughs. I look at him, distracted: is this our
last conversation? Do I care if obscene jokes fill the
book of a writer I've never read? It seems a sad way
to go.

Yet I see, now we're in the park, that I am
investing this hero – for he surely is that: he
embodies risk, deceit, cunning, art – with the same
inability to suffer sadness or depression that once I
placed in my father. Why shouldn't this man, as
lacking in 'human' qualities when it comes to love
as the beast he resembles and admires, still be
capable of knowing the time has come – for now, at
least – to give up the chase? Do women who have
been in thrall to their fathers, refusing to admit a
human weakness in the object of their hidden
desires, invariably attract him? Why, too, shouldn't
abandoning the joy of pursuit bring a recognised

and understood response from the one no longer
sought or loved? Pride and vanity, of course – but I
feel I could do better than, in an imitation of
bouncy Sally, toss my head and look peeved at the
ending that must now come.

Ted sits silent on the wooden bench that looks
out towards the peacocks and down the forked path
where the child trotted with a baby fox, what seems
many years ago. He has said, in the very quiet voice
that means he wants you to listen and absorb, that
he must stay at home. An old man walks by, and I
see Ted's suddenly alert look, as if seeing himself in
the future – or his father, perhaps, who wanted to
escape and was found so fast, so easily, in his little
love-nest by King's Cross.

'What about Windy Gap?' I say.

'Don't,' Ted says. I also see him all at once with
new eyes: his shoulders are stooped and he sits on
the bench like a vagrant, a man who once was
somewhere but now has nowhere to go.

It is growing cold. I still feel irked by having
had to pay the bill at the Portobello ('I've no money
on me today') and I wish I didn't, because it
trivialises everything.

We both rise, and at the gate of Holland Park
we turn to go our separate ways: Ted to a taxi, to
Ken High, and I to Notting Hill.

Spiral Bindings

Back from Scotland, where I gave a huge party to celebrate the publication of *The Bad Sister* and *Wild Nights*, the latter a fantastical account of my family here in the past – so both books are Scottish in origin.

I was happy to be at Glen without the royalty or butlers associated with my elder brother's tenure of the place: Allan Massie came, and Liz Calder from Jonathan Cape in London and Stephen Frears, as well as plenty of friends and Scottish writers. It seems a long time since I tiptoed to the photo albums in the drawing-room, in order to try and subsidise a magazine.

I obviously cannot resist starting something up again. Today, back in London, I mixed champagne and Guinness together to make Black Velvet for the managing director of Faber, Matthew Evans, and his editorial director, Robert McCrum. They came to Julian Rothenstein's work-room, a stone's throw from the old *Bananas* office, and I showed them mock-ups for the first books we shall publish as 'Next Editions': Faber has generously given the money for the project.

The books are spiral-bound and illustrated. Angela Carter is writing *Black Venus* for us, the story of Baudelaire's black mistress in 1940s Paris. There's Mandelstam's *Journey to Armenia* with a new introduction by Chatwin; Elaine Feinstein's poem, *The Feast of Eurydice*, and Harold Pinter writes a play, *Family Voices*, which will make its first appearance in Next Editions. This, along with Liz Lochhead, whom I admire and track down, will make a fine start for the imprint.

Here we are, the following spring, cutting a cake to mark the publication of *Family Voices*, illustrated by Harold's artist friend Guy Vaesen.

Later, there is a party, this time at Thompsons Restaurant. 'We never thought it would happen,' Evans of Faber admits. And there is Angela, the white magician, standing in the doorway, the sun turning her hair to a snowy blaze. She sees me and I come forward to greet her. 'I brought . . . he's a student at . . . UEA . . . ' Angela's words come with difficulty as she propels a young man in my direction. 'This is Kazuo Ishiguro.'

Thompsons fills up and people spill out into the Notting Hill Street. The party goes on.

The Aftermath

I'm walking up Ladbroke Grove, with the north of
the city lying below in a shimmer of pollution, and
the hawthorn blossom bright on the hedges in the
communal gardens on either side of the Grove.

I should be happy; but I am filled with fear:
fear of what I shall hear today; fear of death, of non-
being, of loss and extinction and the void. I think of
the primal fear Ted would have us all return to, the
fear of the dark, of wild animals, the night wind.
And I know this is the fear I am feeling. It is the
first nodding acquaintance with death.

Five days ago I found a lump in my breast;
today, after X-ray and biopsy, the results will be
conveyed to me by Dr Johnston, a GP in Holland
Park Avenue so much shorter than I am that he
barely comes up to the offending part of my
anatomy. This I have heard him describe to a
specialist on the phone as 'she's a big girl', and I feel
no liking for Dr Johnston. The road to death, as I'm
coming to realise, is paved with euphemisms and
banalities, and life's greatest luxury is a freedom
from the familiarity of strangers. But I know I fear,
too, those appurtenances of the modern world
which are a long way from Hughes's primitive
terrors: I fear, should the diagnosis show

malignancy, the great machines, the dinosaurs of radiotherapy I've seen on TV or heard described by friends who've been victims of the Big C. I don't know, on this May morning in Ladbroke Grove, if I have the courage to lie under their Cyclops gaze.

Mandarin Books in Notting Hill Gate is run by the excellent Harry and Mavis, and is the sole bookshop in this part of West London. It is packed with books on politics, with poetry and obscure translations and new novels that never could be found in W. H. Smith. Elaine Feinstein and Angela Carter are already here, when I turn up. They are down by the crowded pay desk and Angela is talking animatedly – as far as her pauses, reconsiderations and sudden intakes of breath permit – to Harry. Elaine waves to me as I'm glimpsed behind a tottering pile of – what else on a day like today? – *Johnny Panic and the Bible of Dreams*, the collection of Plath's writings put together by Hughes. As I wave back to Elaine, preparing already an apology for the lateness of the delivery of the poster advertising their signing, for the shop window, I get the feeling that invariably comes when 'coincidences' present themselves. Why, on this day of all days, have Harry and Mavis chosen to display the book I least want to see?

I turn suddenly as a friend, Francis Wyndham, comes into the shop, an act of solidarity and kindness on his part, a gesture of support for the signing, and my movement gives me the unexpected sight of my own reflection, in the opening and shutting glass door. 'If you see yourself walking towards you, you're done for,' Hughes has told me cheerfully, in the past. Now, here I am – it's only a mirror image, true – apparently inviting death even before it's officially declared to be on the cards. The worst of it is that I appear to have become permanently afflicted by the superstitions and occult beliefs of my time with Ted. The bad-luck feeling has me in its grasp: a fear from the ancient world of spells and curses grips me and won't let go.

I don't have to wait long. The stocky figure of Dr Johnston is the figure that actually walks towards me when I step out onto the pavement, ostensibly in search of customers for signed copies of Elaine's *The Feast of Eurydice* and Angela's *Black Venus*. And I know for sure before he comes up to me, frowning with concern, that this is it: I'm done for. 'You left the number here,' says Dr Johnston, squinting up at me. 'It's bad news.'

THE YEARS OF EVIL FORTUNE

The years of evil fortune begin. Major illness (for me). The death of my eight-year-old daughter's father. The death of my father. My daughter's car accident and broken leg, the death of Marjorie, whom she loved. In the seven years between 1977, when Ted and I first got together, and 1984 the list is terrifying and appears endless.

In 1984, Ted is crowned Poet Laureate. From a verse, again by Yeats: 'Those cheers that can be bought or sold, that office fools have run . . . '

Twice Ted tried to reach me, in the years that followed. The first time, we met late at night in a Notting Hill bar and went back to my house – filled with my family – and talked and talked. The second time, Ted tried to fix another Arvon writing-school visit, this time to the Yorkshire centre, near where Sylvia is buried. He would be there. But, as if obeying the law of the three chances, of which the third is useless, soiled, corrupt, I found myself refusing the offer. I was happy at home now, with the man who'd seen me through the bad times.

The Golden Bowl

I've moved house again, down the road to a small
house with a long garden; and last night, when Ted
rang and suggested dinner, I couldn't see any harm
in meeting him – in North London, as usual. Much
of what I'd been thinking about him surfaced then:
again, as usual, what is revealed is a two-headed
monster, a paragon of good and evil fame.

For Ted has to win. As he runs, he may discard
or lose his most treasured possessions – wife, love,
peace of mind – but he must end at the winning-
post, triumphant, handsome as a god, and the
greatest prize, the golden bowl, must be his. The
trouble is, as he must be aware, a golden bowl, as in
the novel by Henry James, is liable to contain a
hidden crack. In this case, it's the money from the
Plath Estate which is the fault in the treasured prize.
And tonight, in a gloomy restaurant in Camden, I'm
sitting at dinner with Ted and his sister and the
crack gapes open for all to see. For Ted has to go
tomorrow to New York, to attend the court case
concerning the film of Plath's novel *The Bell Jar*.
There is a lot of money at stake – whether he loses
or wins.

'What will become of you if . . . ?' As so often
before, I blurt out the thought uppermost in my
mind, without, in this instance, realising that Ted's

unusual silences and passive demeanour are giving
him the air of a Victorian heroine about to undergo
further ill-treatment at the hands of a husband or
boss. Faced with the might of the American courts,
has Ted transformed into to Jane Eyre, from his
usual part as Mr Rochester? My question is an
unexpected one, for so masterful a man. He looks
balefully across the table at me and I wish I hadn't
spoken.

Instead, we start to talk about Ian Hamilton,
contemporary of Ted's and *his* court case, also in
America. Ian's plan to bounce J. D. Salinger from
his long spell of isolation and write his biography
has misfired badly, due to a law (unknown to
Hamilton) concerning the ownership of the content
of correspondence. However freely the public may
gain access to letters by Salinger, they cannot be
reproduced without the author's permission. And
Salinger has refused permission. There's something
faintly embarrassing about this subject too, though,
with Plath's letters and journals exclusively in Ted's
possession and further disapproval likely if they are
withheld – with more contempt for Ted if they're
published and the royalties start pouring in. It
occurs to me forcibly that Ted has been placed in an
impossible situation by the death of the feminist
icon Sylvia has become, and his 'ownership' of her,
after death: winner though he may strive to be, Ted
cannot win.

Maybe because of this, I direct my thoughts to
the subject of the forthcoming court case, brought
by a woman, formerly a fellow student of Plath's,
who has found herself depicted as a lesbian in the
film. But when I try falteringly to bring up this
topic, I find I am reminded again of a Victorian
novel – or perhaps I've actually returned to that era,
without knowing this is what I was in for when I
said I would join these natives of the Yorkshire
moors for dinner. The very word 'lesbian' seems to
occasion a spasm of hatred in Ted – I've never seen
him look at me this way. And Olwyn, who finds an
opportunity to start on about the 'libbers' who have
promoted her late sister-in-law to such unwelcome
heights, appears to imply that all feminists and the
like are committed lesbians. *If*, like Queen Victoria,
either sibling will allow such a person as a lesbian
to exist, that is.

Now I decide to tough out my indiscretions
and I look straight across at the man who will in two
days' time be in the dock, in the United States, to
protect his late wife's book and his own fortune. He
wears a shifty expression – so I think, at least, until
the arrival of the coffee and the bill announce the
end of dinner, and the beginning of a sense of
impending freedom chases across his features, like
a cloud on a breezy day. He assumes control – 'I'll
see you home,' he tells his sister – and he returns
my gaze at last, with a deliberately assumed roguish

grin. 'I'll run you home afterwards,' he says – and, foolish though it is when there is no competition between the women at the table, I'm unable to prevent myself thinking of Paris, resplendent in his male beauty once more, awarding the golden apple.

All this gold . . . I decide later it's the court case, the damages possibly awarded to the plaintiff who objects to being named a lesbian, the profits and losses that come with the Plath legend, which bring gold to mind. There's scandal, too: I have a strange feeling, as the car hurtles through the empty streets of North London, that Ted, while desperate for privacy and the avoidance of scandal, worships it as he loves gold. It bathes him in a lurid light, which both attracts and repels the women who cluster round him. 'I would have given you those poems for your magazine,' Ted says as we drive along. He has been speaking of verses he has written which have since disappeared. 'They were burnt . . . ' He gives a laugh and I think of the poem 'Burning the Letters' by Plath, which Olwyn gave us to publish when the paper hadn't been going long, and I see both Plath and Hughes, for a minute in the blackness of Regent's Park, surrounded by flames. 'When . . . the girl who burnt my house in Yorkshire set fire to all my papers,' Ted says, and he is still laughing, 'and only the centres of the rooms would take, because of the damp . . . '

He knows and I know he has told me of this

act of revenge before. But it's true the image is a powerful one and I feel I'm being urged to express shock at this scandalous deed. Ted needs to see me excited and shocked. 'And the middles of the rooms fell through, one into the other,' he intones, 'and all those poems went, and letters too . . . '

Ted knows the power of the card that is the myth built around his life and love for Sylvia, his betrayal and desertion. He plays it – and in court, even in the city where he is seen as the murderer of the most worshipped poet of the age, he will be sure to win.

It's August and I'm in Dorset, near enough to the
sea to go there fairly often – though my mother,
who comes to stay with us here shortly, would go
there on a daily basis if she could. The cliffs at West
Bay, crumbling, yellow, precarious yet
indestructible, draw her, as does the sand, tiger-
striped as the tide goes out, leaving laps of darkness
against the drying gold. The waves are tall, too tall,
and I don't like to see myself in my imagination run
to rescue her as they pound in, forcing her up
against the fallen boulders at the cliff's base. What if
there is another rock fall, or a freak wave, a wall of
water that would sweep us both away? But I am full
of fears and she has none. I shall say nothing as she
walks, growing slowly smaller as she moves away
from me, along the treacherous beach towards
Chesil Bank.

I've reached the point in writing about my life
when I arrive in Notting Hill and begin to dream of
starting a magazine. 'Of course I have a set of
Bananas,' Julian Rothenstein says when I call him
from the small sitting-room where children's sandy
feet, trailing in from a visit to the sea, have
deposited the stuff on worn rug and cement floor
underneath. With my toe in white gym shoe I push
sand under the adjacent armchair, and wonder that
I've been here since 1980, the year of the bad luck,

of a house move which came on top of the cancer, of despair and the seeding of my worst fears – probably the reason for my anxiety when my mother or my children walk on the beach at West Bay. I'm grateful to have lived eighteen years since then; indeed, the days of the magazine seem an impossibly long time ago. 'But it's the only set of *Bananas*,' Julian goes on, laughing. 'I don't know why, but it's all we've got.' I know, I think, wincing at the memory of the move from the house in Notting Hill, while undergoing the attentions of the great radiotherapy machines in the basement of Westminster Hospital. There was nowhere to store the hundreds of copies of the magazine. Life was telling us that such frivolities and amusements were no longer on the menu: this was Death: this was real.

And casting my mind back to that house, to the long kitchen and playroom downstairs, with the doll's house at the back, by the window that looks out on the gardens, I remember the evening I came back there with Ted, and turned my foot in the wonky shoes, and how he marched me up and down in the darkness as if trying to persuade himself – and me – that there was really nothing wrong with me at all. He couldn't be responsible for an 'invalid' – especially one who might, like all the other women he had loved, become a corpse. I see him very clearly, and myself as I hobble finally to reach the one working lamp. Then it all fades, except for the voice which picks over words carefully before letting them go out into the world.

I haven't seen Ted, not properly, not to speak to – he was at the memorial service for Stephen Spender at St Martin's-in-the-Fields two years ago and afterwards at the party at the Garrick, but stood all evening with the widow of T. S. Eliot and I didn't go up to him – for at least ten years. I heard from friends last winter that he'd been ill; then, in the summer, that treatment had been successful. I don't believe anything dreadful could ever happen to Ted.

Storms and high winds have brought me strange times. Maybe because I write of Ted – more than most of the rest of the cast of those magazine days, and with a freedom I hadn't expected to come – I find I dream of him nearly every night: lately, with a kind of anguish. This has been a triumphant year for him, with his translation of Ovid and with the publication of *Birthday Letters*. Yet my dreams are all of death. Yesterday, I wrote down the dream that is a replay of our Devon meeting – this after a night in which I sensed him near and holding out his hand, palm upwards, in which a whiteness glowed.

Ted Hughes Remembered

'Ted is very long-distance.' I hear his sister Olwyn's words, and – for no reason that comes instantly, I remember a description I heard somewhere of the wooing of Ted by Assia, Sylvia's dark rival. 'She sent him grasses in an envelope, stones and pebbles, that kind of thing.' I think of the pen, the Mont Blanc I proudly presented to the poet who loves to help children – and women, especially women – to 'find their story', and of the time I went to meet him when he'd had the pen a month or so and had written a poem with it, two sides of a sheet of white paper covered in the markings and crossings of a first draft, like a bird's footprints in snow. What did I do with the poem? He was mildly reproachful at the fact I was angry about something instead: the Australian, the absence of news or phone-calls, the random nature of our communications with each other. To make up for my mood that day, I sent a bottle of black ink through the post to Devon. Thick black ink, which the pen would gobble up and spit out, in poems as hard to decipher as runes.

Why I'm thinking about these things, now twenty years in the past, is because I sat in a restaurant with an old friend, Jay, a year ago almost to the day and Ted came into the conversation –

quite unexpectedly. Jay spoke of illness and death. He's an actor and has lived all his life (or so it seems by now) with Peter, a musician. Peter has been diagnosed with AIDS and is unlikely to make it through the 'festive' season. Jay fights for Peter: he is brave and refuses to allow himself to grieve – yet – but he says, looking at me gravely and without blinking his large, gentle brown eyes: 'I'm going to be very unhappy.'

There's nothing that can be said to this. Peter lies in hospital, but will return home at the end of the week to die. I can only stare across at Jay, who eats little of his salad and toys with his hair, as long as it was when I first knew him back in the '60s, like an adolescent as he speaks. I am full of admiration and pity for this pair who have shown their love for each other with such gallantry and compassion.

'They all go to the same healer,' Jay is now saying. 'I can't say it's doing much good to any of them.'

'What's that?' I'm enfolded in the atmosphere of illness, a climate I'd practically forgotten: despair and fear, hand in hand with the sudden belief in a magical cure. I remember how I was told, after my own cancer was diagnosed, that there was a faith healer in Devon – was his name Ted Cornish? – and that I should go and see him. This from friends of Ted Hughes; and it makes me think of him. I hear a

voice (whose, I don't remember) saying to me: 'He
wrote to you, when he heard you were ill. He was
very upset. But' – and now, as I sit across the little
polished table from Jay, I hardly hear what he is
saying about Peter, and about hospitals, at all – 'but
the letter was found in his jacket pocket. It never
got posted.' Then a silence, followed by a sigh. I
have to wrench myself back to the present, to Jay's
imminent tragedy. Fish comes, coiled round and
guarding a purée of something green. 'Ted is very
interested in healers,' Jay is saying. 'He and Peter
are always conferring.'

'Ted?' I say, surprised, but unsurprised in that
way which seems to accompany any mention of
him: there will always, as in the case of my own
memory of the recommendation of Ted Cornish, be
some coincidence, easily explicable or totally
mysterious, connected with the bringing-up of Ted's
name. 'Yes, he has cancer too,' Jay says. Then he
frowns. 'He doesn't want anyone to know.'

It's now, I suppose, that I begin to grasp the
reality of the nature of time, of Ted's time, 'long-
distance' time, anyway. The news that he is stricken
with cancer pierces me as if it was only last week I
saw him – all the clichés about time and pain come
unbidden to mind as his image presents itself and
refuses to go away.

'How? Where?' I hear myself asking. The
image swells and lingers, of Picasso's dying bull, the

Minotaur in the ring, with the outstretched hands of
young girls fluttering from the stadium. 'Poor Ted,' I
say, so loudly the other tables glance anxiously over
at me. Jay replies he doesn't know which part of
Ted is being eaten by cancer: the news has come
from a writer friend who tutored an Arvon course in
Yorkshire. 'He told us about his weekend at Lumb
Bank – I haven't seen him since then,' Jay says. 'He
thinks very highly of the way people are
encouraged to write at Arvon. Didn't you go there
once?'

I sit on, again unable to reply or listen. Arvon
of all things: it's the very last occasion I want to
hear about, especially now. I remember
Hawthorne's story, *Wakefield*, of the man who went
from his house one day to buy a trivial domestic
object – and didn't return. His wife waited;
sometimes, having taken up residence in an
adjoining street, her spouse came and saw her,
silhouetted behind a blind in the first-floor sitting-
room, pacing. After twenty years he suddenly walks
in again. I understand that story, now: twenty years
is everything and nothing, time means nothing
where Ted is concerned. 'I met Ted,' Jay says, 'at a
grand dinner. He read his poems afterwards; it was
very moving, I must say.'

'Did you like him?' I ask (anything I say
sounds foolish, now).

'Oh yes, I did. We talked about you.' Jay pulls a

strand of hair across his face, as he always does
when embarrassed. He lowers his voice and
mumbles. I have to lean right forward, over the
bright-yellow glasses of wine, to hear what he says.
'Ted said you were going to go off together.'

'Oh – did he?' I don't want to hear this
confidence; so much is returning with a rush and I
need time to digest, sort it out and disperse.

'He said he was frightened. Or alarmed – is
that what he said? Too alarming . . . '

For the first time in what seems an age, I
almost smile.

Back home – after I've made light of this 'dinner-
party remark', as I described it to Jay – I try to give
myself some time to think over what he has told
me. But time is as slippery as ever, and when I try
to ponder his words, all I see are the missed
opportunities or the refused invitations: the
teaching course in Yorkshire Arvon, also at Lumb
Bank, which he organised for me to go to and I
turned down, and where he would have been; a
dinner here, a party there, all openings for a
renewal. Real time – the here and now in which I
must think over what Jay has told me – has become
fatally overlaid with the past.

Then, waking this morning, I see and know
the truth behind words – words which I had
dismissed as a desire on Ted's part to break a long

silence by talking to someone who knows me. The truth is, no-one has ever matched up to Sylvia, for Ted. He gave her his heart, and he has spent thirty years trying to find it again, in an odyssey that has taken him from 'Russia' to 'Australia' to 'Scotland' – and back to Devon again. He has been, as he said to me when dropping me back in Notting Hill after going to his flat, as faithful to his first mate as the greylag goose.

October 28th. Elaine has just called, to say Ted died last night.

Everyone – apart, obviously, from close friends and family – stunned by the news.

Ted's face keeps appearing in flashes at the end of programmes, on TV. Film of swollen rivers – the rivers he loved – in a dark landscape. Weirdly, the main story is of an escaped lion in Devon; children are interviewed saying they're 'not really frightened'. No-one knows where the lion came from, and the story is dropped after a couple of days. All I can keep thinking is that Ted died on the day after Sylvia's birthday. It's as if he made himself hold out till then. I never discovered the secret I always felt he nursed within, without really wanting to – if one there is. In all the years since we knew each other there were frequent new revelations

from the Plath 'fantasia', as Ted described it. Among **229**
them was the fact that one of Sylvia's journals was
destroyed by him and the other 'disappeared'.

Were these the burnt diaries of my early
dream, the diaries containing the truth of Ted's past
which would set him free? His own account came
in *Birthday Letters*, in the spring. Now, with his
death, it jumps up the bestseller charts. He would
have shrugged – and laughed.

A short while later and I find I'm still writing about Ted, as if he is alive and could read what I've written. I catch myself wondering if he will suddenly get in touch again.

In the communal gardens, an hour or so before it grew dark, and I walked round with Jean, the Yorkshire terrier, on her lead. I was thinking of the last communication I had from Ted, in March this year, when I'd sent him a copy of the memoir about my family and my early years, *Strangers*. I wasn't sure then if he was ill or well, and sent only a brief note with the book, congratulating him on *Ovid*.

The card that came back shows in colour a great hooked salmon fly, a 'Hairy Mary', as its italic label proclaims it. 'Windy Gap etc.' says the very black ink, the writing as well defined as when I first came to know it. The message continues: 'I don't think I ever got to the Gap. But since we last met I've got to know Scotland better, and I know I'm in the wrong land.'

It's when I'm standing in the middle of the communal gardens smiling at the thought of the card – at the Tedness of the card, with its hint of a coded message as well as the rueful apology for failing to reach the road to Paradise (Yeats) or the old woman with her promise that 'the best years are

yet to come' (folk, attributed by Hughes to Burns) –
that I see the fox. It's a bright afternoon, without a
hint of the night that will come in less than an hour
. . . The gardens are, unusually, completely empty.
Yet I only see the fox because the lead goes slack:
the terrier stands stock still and refuses to move.

The odd thing about the fox, as I register at
last, is that its coat is grey. Yet it most certainly *is* a
fox, with a fox's face. Elderly, perhaps – after standing
and staring back at me it goes off with a slight limp
into the bushes. It's a dog fox – almost as tall, as I
try to remember it on a visit to the zoo, as a wolf.

I walk round the box hedge that separates the
path from the central part of the gardens. I know
where I'm going, and this time the terrier comes
with me obediently.

I stop by the back gate to the house where I
used to live – not the house with the basement
where my foot overturned and I limped back to the
sofa, pretending no harm was done, to Ted, but the
house I moved to in the year of evil fortune, in
1980, a house that was going to bring in badly
needed revenue, as it had rooms ready to let. (In
the event, my family filled every inch of the place.)

The fox is standing there, by the open back
gate, a few feet away through laurel and
rhododendron. I look at it; it looks unblinking back
at me. Then I go home, across the gardens to my
flat.